PN 1590 .B5 S65 1999

Slide, Anthony.

Actors on red alert

FILMMAKERS SERIES
edited by
ANTHONY SLIDE

1. *James Whale,* by James Curtis. 1982
2. *Cinema Stylists,* by John Belton. 1983
3. *Harry Langdon,* by William Schelly. 1982
4. *William A. Wellman,* by Frank Thompson. 1983
5. *Stanley Donen,* by Joseph Casper. 1983
6. *Brian De Palma,* by Michael Bliss. 1983
7. *J. Stuart Blackton,* by Marian Blackton Trimble. 1985
8. *Martin Scorsese and Michael Cimino,* by Michael Bliss. 1985
9. *Franklin J. Schaffner,* by Erwin Kim. 1985
10. *D. W. Griffith and the Biograph Company,* by Cooper C. Graham et al. 1985
11. *Some Day We'll Laugh: An Autobiography,* by Esther Ralston. 1985
12. *The Memoirs of Alice Guy Blaché,* 2nd ed., trans. by Roberta and Simone Blaché. 1996
13. *Leni Riefenstahl and Olympia,* by Cooper C. Graham. 1986
14. *Robert Florey,* by Brian Taves. 1987
15. *Henry King's America,* by Walter Coppedge. 1986
16. *Aldous Huxley and Film,* by Virginia M. Clark. 1987
17. *Five American Cinematographers,* by Scott Eyman. 1987
18. *Cinematographers on the Art and Craft of Cinematography,* by Anna Kate Sterling. 1987
19. *Stars of the Silents,* by Edward Wagenknecht. 1987
20. *Twentieth Century-Fox,* by Aubrey Solomon. 1988
21. *Highlights and Shadows: The Memoirs of a Hollywood Cameraman,* by Charles G. Clarke. 1989
22. *I Went That-a-Way: The Memoirs of a Western Film Director,* by Harry L. Fraser; edited by Wheeler Winston Dixon and Audrey Brown Fraser. 1990
23. *Order in the Universe: The Films of John Carpenter,* by Robert C. Cumbow. 1990
24. *The Films of Freddie Francis,* by Wheeler Winston Dixon. 1991

Actors on Red Alert

*Career Interviews with
Five Actors and Actresses
Affected by the Blacklist*

Anthony Slide

Filmmakers Series, No. 67

The Scarecrow Press, Inc.
Lanham, Maryland, and London
1999

SCARECROW PRESS, INC.

Published in the United States of America
by Scarecrow Press, Inc.
4720 Boston Way
Lanham, Maryland 20706

4 Pleydell Gardens, Folkestone
Kent CT20 2DN, England

British Library Cataloguing in Publication Information Available

Library of Congress Cataloging-in-Publication Data

Slide, Anthony.
    Actors on red alert : career interviews with five actors and
actresses affected by the blacklist / Anthony Slide.
        p.   cm. — (Filmmakers series ; no. 67)
    Filmography: p.
    Includes index.
    ISBN 0-8108-3649-1 (cloth : alk. paper)
    1. Blacklisting of entertainers—United States.   2. Motion picture
actors and actresses—United States—Interviews. I. Title. II. Series
PN1590.B5S65   1999
791.43' 028' 092273—dc21   99-19675
                                                                CIP

∞™ The paper used in this publication meets the minimum requirements of
American National Standard for Information Sciences—Permanence of
Paper for Printed Library Materials, ANSI/NISO Z39.48–1992.
Manufactured in the United States of America.

Contents

INTRODUCTION

On June 7, 1938, under a resolution offered by Martin Dies of Texas, the House of Representatives established the House Committee on UnAmerican Activities, more commonly known as the House UnAmerican Activities Committee or HUAC. Thus was the foundation laid for the blacklist of the late 1940s and 1950s, which most publicly affected the Hollywood film and television community, but which, in reality, infiltrated all areas of American society and culture. The committee began its insidious work in earnest in 1947, under the chairmanship of J. Parnell Thomas of New Jersey, when an investigation began "to determine the extent of Communist infiltration of the Hollywood motion picture industry."

Witnesses were labeled by the committee as either "friendly" or "unfriendly," and among the former group were actors Gary Cooper, Adolphe Menjou, Robert Montgomery, George Murphy, Ronald Reagan, and Robert Taylor. Speaking of the Screen Actors Guild (SAG) before the committee in Washington, D.C., on October 22, 1947, Robert Taylor commented, "It seems to me that at meetings, especially meetings of the general membership of the Guild, there is always a certain group of actors and actresses whose every action would indicate to me that, if they are not Communists, they are working awfully hard to be Communists."[1] He went on to single out Howard Da Silva and Karen Morley, the first actors to be "named" to the committee.

Of Robert Taylor and his colleagues, Dalton Trumbo wrote in *The Time of the Toad.*

> The actors, successful artists all and therefore without private axes to grind, appeared to speak from the deepest wellsprings of patriotism. True, their testimony was prepared by others and carefully rehearsed in advance with Mr. Robert Stripling, committee investigator. But they were eager participants in the

show, and their performances seemed to reflect a solemn conviction that their accused fellow-workers were so actively engaged in revolutionary foment that their violent overthrow of the government constituted an imminent peril.[2]

The initial hearings concluded on October 31, 1947, with the citation for contempt of Congress of ten filmmakers who refused to divulge their past or present political affiliations. This group—Alvah Bessie, Herbert Biberman, Lester Cole, Edward Dmytryk, Ring Lardner Jr., John Howard Lawson, Albert Maltz, Samuel Ornitz, Adrian Scott, and Dalton Trumbo—became known as "The Hollywood Ten." Dmytryk subsequently cooperated with the committee and, in 1951, identified various individuals, including Lloyd Bridges, Sterling Hayden, Marc Lawrence, and Larry Parks, as members of the Communist Party.

In response to the hearings, the Committee for the First Amendment was formed, with five hundred members of the film community stating they were

> disgusted and outraged by the continuing attempt of the House Committee on UnAmerican Activities to smear the motion picture industry.
> We hold that these hearings are morally wrong, because:
> Any investigation into the political beliefs of the individual is contrary to the basic principles of our democracy;
> Any attempt to curb freedom of expression and to set arbitrary standards of Americanism is in itself disloyal to both the spirit and the letter of the Constitution.

On October 26 and November 2, 1947, the ABC radio network broadcast two surveys, directed by Norman Corwin, on behalf of the committee, and including statements from more than sixty members of the industry. On October 29, 1947, twenty-nine members of the Committee for the First Amendment presented a petition in Washington, D.C. That group included Lauren Bacall, Humphrey Bogart, Geraldine Brooks, Richard Conte, June Havoc, Sterling Hayden, Paul Henreid, Marsha Hunt, Danny Kaye, Gene Kelly, Evelyn Keyes, and Jane Wyatt.

As anti-Communist hysteria swept the country, the Committee for the First Amendment was quickly (and quietly) disbanded, although a new group, the Committee of One Thousand, appeared briefly, with members including Deanna

Durbin, Florence Eldridge, and Fredric March continuing the campaign. Many of those who were members of the Committee for the First Amendment faced blacklisting or, at the least, so-called graylisting. Others were forced to make public penance, as, for example, with Humphrey Bogart's writing "I'm No Communist" in the March 1948 issue of *Photoplay*.

Squaring off against the Committee for the First Amendment was a group calling itself the Motion Picture Alliance for the Preservation of American Ideals. Formed in 1944, the alliance's president was for many years John Wayne, and on its executive committee were actors Ward Bond, Gary Cooper, Adolphe Menjou, Pat O'Brien, Kane Richmond, and Robert Taylor.

This was not the first time that actors and actresses had been politicized, but it was, arguably, the first occasion on which performers were forced into angry conflict one against the other. In 1933 a pioneering group of actors had led the fight for unionization and the establishment of the Screen Actors Guild. Actors and actresses from both sides of the political spectrum had been united in what they considered a just and viable cause back then, including Lew Ayres, Mary Brian, James Gleason, Boris Karloff, Ralph Morgan, Alan Mowbray, Ginger Rogers, Gloria Stuart, Lyle Talbot, Fay Wray, and Robert Young. Ralph Morgan had been the first president of SAG, but he was quickly succeeded by the better-known and more influential Eddie Cantor, a dedicated campaigner against Nazi Germany and the German-American Bund. By its boycott of the 1936 Academy Awards presentation, the guild forced the Academy of Motion Picture Arts and Sciences to remove itself from the position of a bargaining unit for talent. The following year, the first SAG contract was signed with thirteen producers, guaranteeing a minimum wage for both actors and extras; and in 1945, SAG was actively involved in the jurisdictional dispute between International Alliance of Theatrical Stage Employees, Moving Picture Technicians, Artists and Allied Crafts and the Conference of Studio Unions.

Whatever liberal stance the Screen Actors Guild might have adopted in the 1930s, it was gone by 1950, when, in October of that year, the guild drafted a loyalty oath for signature by all its members. In 1953 the guild added a paragraph to its bylaws, stating,

No person who is a member of the Communist Party or of any

other organization seeking to overthrow the government of the United States by force and violence shall be eligible for membership in the Screen Actors Guild. The application for Guild membership shall contain the following statement to be signed by the applicant: "I am not now and will not become a member of the Communist Party, nor of any other organization that seeks to overthrow the government of the United States by force and violence."

Gale Sondergaard was a prominent Hollywood character actress and also the wife of Herbert Biberman, one of "The Hollywood Ten." When she was subpoenaed to appear before HUAC in October 1951, she wrote to SAG:

I most earnestly and fraternally ask the Board to consider the implications of the forthcoming hearing. A blacklist already exists. It may now be widened. It may ultimately be extended to include any freedom-loving nonconformist or any member of a particular race or any member of a union—or anyone.

Her plea for help fell on deaf ears, with a spokesman for SAG responding,

The Guild as a labor union will fight against any secret blacklist created by any group of employers. On the other hand, if any actor by his own actions outside of union activities has so offended American public opinion that he has made himself unsaleable at the box office, the Guild cannot and would not want to force any employer to hire him. That is the individual actor's personal responsibility and it cannot be shifted to his union.

Leading the local attack on the so-called Communists within the film industry was a frustrated playwright named Myron C. Fagan (October 31, 1887 to May 12, 1972). He was the author of *Thieves Paradise,* billed as "the first play to expose the fiendishness of Communism behind the 'iron curtain,'" which opened in Hollywood at the Las Palmas Theatre on December 26, 1947, in front of an audience that included Adolphe Menjou, Robert Montgomery, and Ginger Rogers. Fagan claimed the leading man, Howard Johnson, was "terrorized into a nervous breakdown" by "Reds" within the Hollywood community, and that same group had tried to prevent the play's reopening at the El Patio Theatre in Hollywood on April 12, 1948.

Obsessed with his theory of a Communist conspiracy, sure in his belief that he had been blacklisted by "Hollywood moguls who loved profit more than patriotism," in 1948 Fagan was instrumental in the founding of the Cinema Educational Guild, Inc., to publish such reactionary tracts as *Red Treason in Hollywood* (1949). The latter contains a listing of performers identified by Fagan as "Stalin's Stars," among whose number are Eddie Cantor, Howard Da Silva, Bette Davis, Olivia de Havilland, Albert Dekker, Melvyn Douglas, Florence Eldridge, Jose Ferrer, John Garfield, Rita Hayworth, Paul Henreid, Katharine Hepburn, Rose Hobart, Lena Horne, Gene Kelly, Alexander Knox, Burt Lancaster, Fredric March, Larry Parks, Gregory Peck, Ann Revere, Edward G. Robinson, Paul Robeson, Sylvia Sidney, Gale Sondergaard, Gloria Stuart, Franchot Tone, and Orson Welles.

Myron C. Fagan was also behind publication, in June 1950, of *Red Channels*, the "bible" for producers in the film, radio, and television industries (with the emphasis strongly on the last two mediums), listing all those identified as Communists or Communist sympathizers whose involvement in any entertainment project would make it unacceptable to a silent and unidentified majority of Americans. One hundred fifty names are listed in *Red Channels*, almost half of whom are actors and actresses, the best known being Edith Atwater, Mady Christians, Lee J. Cobb, Howard Da Silva, Alfred Drake, Howard Duff, Jose Ferrer, John Garfield, Will Geer, Ruth Gordon, Rose Hobart, Judy Holliday, Marsha Hunt, Sam Jaffe, Aline McMahon, Margo, Burgess Meredith, Zero Mostel, Edward G. Robinson, Gale Sondergaard, Lionel Stander, Paul Stewart, Sam Wanamaker, and Orson Welles.

It took a full decade for a listing in *Red Channels* to cease to have relevance, and at the end of that decade, Myron C. Fagan and his Cinema Educational Guild, Inc. was still active. It was not until 1961 that the California State Senate Fact-Finding Subcommittee on UnAmerican Activities branded Fagan's listings of alleged Hollywood Communists as "sheer nonsense."

That same year, J. Edgar Hoover also criticized Fagan and others, writing,

There exists today in our land a vital "rift" which the communists are exploiting. Unfortunately, this involves certain people across the country who engage in reckless charges against one another. The label of "communist" is too often indiscriminately attached to those whose views differ from the majority. Those whose lives are not lived according to what one segment of society might decree to be the "norm" are too frequently challenged as "Reds."[3]

To Fagan and others, the Actors' Laboratory, or Actors' Lab, was the center of communism in Hollywood. Founded in May 1941, the Actors' Lab had its origins in New York's Group Theatre and the Federal Theatre Project, and was a successor to the Hollywood Theatre Alliance. By the late 1940s its executive board consisted of chairman Roman Bohnen, vice chairman Sam Levene, treasurer Larry Parks, executive secretary Rose Hobart, and John Berry, J. Edward Bromberg, Phil Brown, Morris Carnovsky, Hume Cronin, Jules Dassin, Edward Dmytryk, Jody Gilbert, Ruth Nelson, S. Sylvan Simon, Art Smith, Gloria Stuart, Mary Tarcai, and Irene Tedrow.

As its members faced subpoenas from the House UnAmerican Activities Committee, the Actors' Lab responded with a full-page advertisement in the February 18, 1948, edition of Daily Variety. It refused to enter into a "mud-slinging" contest with Senator Tenney and announced it would "stand on our record as a free theatre and an *acting school* approved for veterans." But Tenney and his committee had powerful allies in government. In 1948 the IRS revoked the tax-exempt status of the Actors' Lab, and the following year, the Lab was forced to end its involvement in the veterans' training program. By 1950 it was all over, and the Actors' Lab had ceased to exist, its membership constituting the first major group of actors and actresses to experience the power and the wrath of the House UnAmerican Activities Committee.

It was not until one year later that the committee began a major attack on the Hollywood acting fraternity. Some performers were forced to compromise themselves in order to survive. Some hurt only their pride by claiming, as did Lucille Ball, that membership in the Communist Party in the 1930s was simply in order to placate a harmless relative, in Ball's case her socialist grandfather. Others found themselves subpoenaed by a committee, now headed by John S. Wood of Georgia, and were forced to name their colleagues.

Larry Parks was the first to testify, on March 21, 1951, and he identified a group of actors as fellow Communist Party members: Roman Bohnen, J. Edward Bromberg, Morris Carnovsky, Lee J. Cobb, Lloyd Gough, Victor Killian, Karen Morley, Anne Revere, Gale Sondergaard, and Dorothy Tree. Despite his "coming clean" before the committee, Parks found himself blacklisted and denounced by the right wing, led by gossip columnist Hedda Hopper, John Wayne, and the Los Angeles Times. Other actors followed Parks to the witness stand: Sterling Hayden on April 10, 1951; Fred Keating on July 19, 1951; Lloyd Bridges on *October 22, 1951* (the names that he gave the committee have never been made public); Leon Janney on February 13, 1952; Paul Marion on October 2, 1952; and Lee J. Cobb on June 2, 1953.

Of all those blacklisted or graylisted as a result of the work of the House UnAmerican Activities Committee, it is the actors and actresses who, arguably, suffered the most. Their faces were familiar to the American public, and, unlike directors or writers, they could not work under a pseudonym. There were some, as Victor S. Navasky has written, who "seemed to die of blacklist."[4] The acting community lost Mady Christians in 1951, and J. Edward Bromberg, John Garfield, and Canada Lee in 1952. Phil Loeb committed suicide in 1955.

Some actors and actresses fleeing Hollywood and the blacklist found work on the New York stage, which remained relatively untouched by the antics of the House UnAmerican Activities Committee. Many of those fleeing the blacklist went to England, where they were labeled "refugees," and where the press had earlier denounced the committee hearings. The Manchester Guardian (October 30, 1947) asked the obvious question, "Since even in the United States Communism is not illegal, what possible reason *can be found for say*ing that no film director or film actor can be a Communist?" The New Statesman and Nation (November 1, 1947) commented,

> There must be thousands of highly respected American citizens in many walks of life who are *wondering how far they are safe*, if any Adolphe Menjou may be called to the witness-box to make slanderous statements about anyone whose past or political opinions he dislikes.

The London Evening Standard (October 28, 1947) editorialized,

> The Hollywood investigations now being conducted by the Congress Committee on un-American activities are only the latest stop on a witch-burning progress whose torch the Committee has been carrying through the Union. To what depths of intolerance have its members sunk!

One London home in which the refugees of the blacklist found warmth and support was that of former American film star Constance Cummings and her playwright-screenwriter husband Benn Levy, who was later a Labour member of Parliament. As Cummings recalls,

> The first I knew of it was when Paul Draper and Larry Adler came over. They were among the first. And then one began to hear about it. Benn spoke out about it, and so did I. We never stopped shooting our mouths off about it.[5]

Benn Levy helped a few refugees financially, and both he and his wife tried to get them work. The blacklist did not become a personal issue for Constance Cummings. "If it had," she comments,

> I think I would have written off America. But we did go back and forth all the time. I never had any trouble about it.

It was an actor, Kirk Douglas, who helped end the blacklist when, in 1960, he gave screen credit to Dalton Trumbo, one of "The Hollywood Ten," on his production of *Spartacus*. And it was another actor, Robert Vaughn, who helped Americans to understand the full historical implications of the blacklist with his book, *Only Victims: A Study of Show Business Blacklisting* (G. P. Putnam's Sons, 1972).

✳ ✳ ✳

Only Victims is just one of many fine volumes written on the history of the House UnAmerican Activities Committee and blacklisting in the Hollywood community. This present volume utilizes blacklisting and graylisting as the links holding together the lives and careers of five very disparate actors and actresses. Each was affected in some way by what took place fifty years ago. Two were subpoenaed. One named names. Two were forced to re-create their careers in Europe. For the first time, these five actors and actresses—Phil Brown, Rose Hobart, Marsha Hunt, Marc Lawrence, and Doris Nolan—discuss their lives and careers in considerable detail. What they have to say makes fascinating reading, even for those perhaps unfamiliar with the names of the subjects of these interviews. All are remarkably bright and intelligent human beings, very open in terms of what they have to say, unafraid to speak out on issues and against those who wronged them in the past, but nonetheless still unwilling to name names when it comes to the House UnAmerican Activities Committee and its prying questions.

Notes

1. Quoted in Eric Bentley, ed., *Thirty Years of Treason: Excerpts from Hearings before the House Committee on UnAmerican Activities, 1938–1968* (New York: Viking Press, 1971), p. 137.

2. Dalton Trumbo, *The Time of the Toad* (Los Angeles: Hollywood Ten, 1949), p. 11.

3. Published in *Screen Actor* (June/July 1961).

4. Victor S. Navasky, *Naming Names* (New York: Viking Press, 1980), p. 340.

5. Interview with Anthony Slide, September 12, 1997.

INTERVIEWS

PHIL BROWN

Phil Brown's name may not be a familiar one, but his face is instantly recognizable in more than a dozen films from the 1940s in which he plays the guy who never got the girl. A new generation of filmgoers knows him for a small but important role in *Star Wars* (1977). He was an amiable actor whose likability easily comes across on screen. Even in a small part, such as the drunken businessman in Joseph Losey's *The Romantic Englishwoman* (1975), he stamps his personality on the scene. Losey concentrates on close-ups of Brown's face and captures an impish quality, which obviously must have been appealing to directors three decades earlier.

Born in Cambridge, Massachusetts, on April 30, 1916—his father was a doctor and his mother a nurse—Phil Brown began his professional acting career after graduation from Stanford University in 1937. His first job on Broadway was as a dancer in *Everywhere I Roam* by Arnold Sundgaard and Marc Connelly, which opened at the National Theatre on December 29, 1938, and ran for a mere thirteen performances. This was followed by appearances in the Group Theatre productions of *My Heart's in the Highlands* (1939), *Thunder Rock* (1939), *Heavenly Express* (1940), and *Night Music* (1940). When the Group Theatre disbanded, Phil Brown wandered out to Los Angeles, making his film debut in *I Wanted Wings* (1941) and becoming heavily involved in the Actors' Lab.

Brown was briefly in the army from 1942 through 1943, and on December 26, 1941, he married Virginia (Ginny) Sharpe, by whom he has two sons, Kevin (born 1943) and Jed (born 1945). When the couple settled in London in the 1950s, they took up residence in a houseboat on the river Thames—Brown has a natural affinity for boats—and Ginny Brown wrote of their experiences in *Swans at My Window* (Heinemann, 1960).

As early as December 16, 1946, Brown signed a contract with

RKO as an actor-director, but it was not until 1951 that he had the opportunity to be a solo director with *The Harlem Globetrotters*, shot in twelve days for Columbia at a cost of $250,000. The film stars Thomas Gomez as Abe Saperstein in the story of an all-American honor student (Billy Brown) who joins the Harlem Globetrotters, faces emotional problems as he marries his sweetheart (Dorothy Dandridge), injures his knee, and is fired, only to return, a chastened player, to help his team win. *The Hollywood Reporter* (October 17, 1951) described the film as "beautifully directed," while *Daily Variety* (October 17, 1951) commented, "Making an ace debut as a screen director is ex-actor and dialogue director Phil Brown, who has captured all of the script's human qualities in great style." The production is unusual as an early all-black basketball drama, directed by a white American, and one deserving of wider attention today.

Unfortunately, the film's success coincided with Brown's blacklisting. His was a subtle ostracism from the film industry in that Brown was not listed in *Red Channels* and did not appear before the House UnAmerican Activities Committee, but he was labeled a liberal and, therefore, a possible Communist, primarily because of his involvement with the Actors' Lab. Brown was forced to leave in 1952 for London—where he had starred on stage in 1948 in *The Glass Menagerie*—and to return to acting. The blacklist followed Brown to the United Kingdom, as he notes in our interview. He had been working with Douglas Fairbanks Jr. in *Douglas Fairbanks Jr. Presents the Rheingold Theatre*—he was seen in *My Favorite Aunt*, first aired on July 22, 1953—when actor-producer Fairbanks was told not to use Brown in any future programs. The premature report of Phil Brown's death in 1975 in various reference works did not exactly help the actor's career.

After eventually deciding to retire, Phil Brown moved back to Los Angeles with his wife, Ginny. The couple live in a sprawling and friendly tract home in North Hollywood, where our interview took place.

ANTHONY SLIDE: How would you characterize the parts you played?

PHIL BROWN: I began playing small parts of course, and then, when I got into something that was sizable, I was always playing the guy who didn't get the girl. A, because I wasn't high enough up the ladder to be a leading man, and B, because I guess it was just something about my personality that I was the guy who didn't get the girl. And I didn't get a lot of girls. I didn't get Jean Arthur, Jeanne Crain, Hedy Lamarr, and Claudette Colbert.

SLIDE: At some point did you consciously start going after these roles?

BROWN: No, I never went after any role. My whole life in Hollywood was centered around the Actors' Laboratory, this little theatre behind Schwab's Drugstore, where we worked for nothing. You see, when the Group Theatre folded in New York, a lot of us who were members of the Group drifted out here because it was a place to earn a living and because it was psychologically uncomfortable to have this group of actors, who had worked and worked and worked together for years, disappear. To stay in the same city was just difficult. So a lot of us just drifted out here, and we founded this place called the Actors' Laboratory. That was really my life, but it didn't earn money. I earned money in the picture business. I had an agent. He would get me a job. I would take it and do it, and go back to the Lab.

SLIDE: You graduated from Stanford in 1937 and then moved to New York to be an actor.

BROWN: Well, I went to New York under odd circumstances. I met a man called Bill Watts, who was a director with the WPA [Work Projects Administration] in San Francisco, through connections with the San Francisco theatre. Through a girl I was in love with—all my life was girls. He was going to New York to work on a film with two very famous documentary filmmakers named Paul Strand and Leo Hurwitz, who had founded Frontier Films. They were in the process of doing a film called *Native Land*. They needed a dogsbody on this, and I was the dogsbody. I worked that summer on *Native Land*. I carried cameras. I was the dummy they threw out of the back of a moving truck, rolled down the hill, etc.

Actually, I wanted to go to New York because I had heard about this Group Theatre. I had heard that it was very progressive theatre, and I was somewhat interested—not overly—in the Stanislavsky approach to acting, of which they were the most famous proponents in this country. The thing that interested me really was that they said they wanted a theatre at which the actors got paid all the time. This was an idea that appealed to me.

SLIDE: Had you already been an actor?

BROWN: I was an actor at Stanford. Oh yes. I played a dozen leading roles and directed at the Community Playhouse and so on. I had some interest in acting, but I concentrated at Stanford on scenic design. Working on *Native Land* was a way of getting to New York, earning a very small amount of pay, and Bill Watts was vaguely connected with the Group Theatre, so I began to have a sort of "in." To get into the Group Theatre was impossible for young people. You just hung around and got acquainted with the other people in the Group. Eventually, if you were lucky, they cast you. And they did cast me in a small role. The Group Theatre used to have summer camps, as it were, to work on their craft in general and to prepare plays for the next season, and I went away with them to a place called Smithtown. That was the last Group summer. After this, they disbanded the Group Theatre.

SLIDE: Were you always left wing? Was your family left wing?

BROWN: No. My family are Republicans, Quakers as well. I'll tell you how it began. I was in love at Stanford with a girl named Mary, who was a year or two ahead of me. She was working at a place called the San Francisco Theatre Union, a left-wing theatre, very small. They did the first production of *Of Mice and Men*. They were working in a funny little place that used to be a church, a crazy old building with enormous ceilings. And I went up there to help on the fixing-up of this theatre. I was the only guy who would climb up a thirty-foot ladder and hang the spotlights. I thought this would put me in good with Mary, but I didn't succeed because she was in love with a guy who was with the ambulance corps in Spain. That was a dead end for me. But she intrigued me with the Group Theatre, where she had been an apprentice years before. She was a Communist, I believe. She didn't try to recruit me, but she began to interest me in the left. So I came to the left through a girl.

SLIDE: It sounds rather as if you became left wing in order to meet girls.

BROWN: That's right. I became an anti-Fascist because I saw

there were fellows called Hitler and Mussolini and Franco, and they were totalitarians. And as a Quaker . . . I don't know whether you know anything about Quakers, but the Quakers are the most democratic people in the world. I began to see that fascism was a terrible thing, and the only people who were doing anything about it in those early stages were the Communists and the left wing people. The Group Theatre was not Communist but left wing.

SLIDE: Did you sincerely believe that left-wing theatre groups could actually make a difference? The groups are so small, and they are preaching to a converted audience.

BROWN: True. My left-wing activities were outside the theatre. For example, one of the most important ones was an outfit called Theatre Arts Committee. We did a thing called *Cabaret Tac*, which was a group of Broadway people, most of them big stars, who put together a political cabaret to raise money to send ambulances to Spain. Roosevelt had forbidden the sending of American arms, but we were allowed to send ambulances. So we would do these political cabarets— sketches, songs, dances—every Sunday night for that winter. That was a kind of left-wing, anti-Fascist activity, if you like, that interested me and in which I participated. One of the hard things to explain is that I am really apolitical. I was anti-Fascist, yes, but I didn't like the idea of the secrecy of communism. I've never been interested in being a Democrat or a Republican. I'm apolitical. My mind is against certain forms of repression, and I'm against racism and all kinds of things. I'm against things more than I'm for them. I express myself in that way. Also, it's kind of insidious. You get involved with a whole group of people, and you begin to do things that they're doing. Again, it was girls.

I was in my first show on Broadway as a dancer. A complete faker. But I got a job as a dancer because I knew how to do work movements. Male dancers didn't know how to use a shovel or a sledgehammer. When I went to this audition, I immediately got a job. It was about Johnny Appleseed and called *Everywhere I Roam*. And there was this most beautiful girl in the world, named Dorothy Berg, who was a Martha Graham dancer. I just fell in love with her on the spot that first day. I had to get into that show, and I did get into that show.

Dorothy was a world-famous dancer and she was left wing. They came to her and asked whether she would do the choreography for a number, "Picket-Line Priscilla," which was to be sung by Beatrice Kay, in *Cabaret Tac*. Well boy, I got into that group! And all of a sudden I'm doing choreography with a world-famous dancer, whom I was in love with. Somebody asked Danny Kaye's wife, Sylvia Fine, to compose another song, "The Curse of the Silk Chemise," which was anti-Japanese, telling you not to buy silk from Japan.

SLIDE: What was the reaction of the established Broadway stars to the Group Theatre? Did they despise it?

BROWN: Oh yes. The Group was looked down on by the old-style independent actors. You see, in those days, there were two definite schools. There were people who talked and talked and talked, like Harold Clurman, who thought and studied, and so on. And then the great majority of Broadway actors who said, "There's nothing to talk about—just get on with it." You don't talk about it. You just act.

SLIDE: As you got older, did you switch over to the other group in terms of your thoughts on acting?

BROWN: My understanding of the Stanislavsky approach is that there is nothing rigid about it at all, which is why I disliked, and still do dislike, Lee Strasberg. You do this! You do that! It's wrong. He was a terrible, terrible man. I met him but I never had anything to do with him. Clurman I could stand. Clurman just talked. He had verbal diarrhea. He could talk for hours and hours and hours. My understanding of the Stanislavsky approach is that he laid down certain guidelines to make you think, and along these lines, you worked out your own scheme of how you approached acting. The ones that you wanted, that you felt useful, you used, and the ones you didn't, you didn't. That's how I behaved, and that's how I've always behaved. A lot of the stuff in the Stanislavsky approach, I just couldn't stand.

SLIDE: When the Group Theatre disbanded, was there a conscious effort by the members to move to Los Angeles?

BROWN: No. It just happened. Some had been here before. Lee Cobb had been here before. People just drifted in this direction. I think a lot of it was that it was painful to be around in New York and have no Group.

SLIDE: The Actors' Lab didn't exist before you moved here?

BROWN: No. The Actors' Lab began in a rather odd sort of way. The Group Theatre and any Stanislavsky people always wanted to teach, and to teach themselves, even as grown, experienced actors. They liked to do scenes and perform, not necessarily making any money out of it. People like J. Edward Bromberg formed a tiny group to hold some classes, first in a live theatre on Hollywood Boulevard, and then, eventually, we got our own place, above a cafe on Franklin Avenue. The Group Theatre was a very well known organization, and so lots of young people in Hollywood heard about these classes and came to participate in them. It just grew. It just gradually grew.

SLIDE: Why Los Angeles? It has no theatre tradition.

BROWN: Employment for all of us. That's why we moved here. We were here to make money to live. This was life on the side, but it was a most important life for most of us. Since we worked so sporadically in pictures anyway, freelance, our important concentration and total emotional life was in the Lab and its good.

SLIDE: You came out here in 1940. Did it take you a long time to get a film role?

BROWN: I had been out here once before. I got a job from New York. William Morris got me a job in a film called *I Wanted Wings*. I came out here, and then I went back. That was my first job, a foot in the door, something I could talk about. It wasn't a big part, but it was a reasonable role, one of the many airmen.

SLIDE: Mitchell Leisen was the director.

BROWN: [laughs] Yes, he was.

SLIDE: How did he compare to a stage director?

BROWN: He was all right, an ordinary, hack director. He was an intelligent man. You just gradually learned what it was like to work on a film, and to work on a film is so boring, as you must know. I learned a lot, I'm sure.

SLIDE: As somebody who had been with the Group Theatre, did you tend to despise a director like Mitchell Leisen?

BROWN: No, I didn't. Of the directors I worked with, some I liked and some I didn't. Some I thought were useful. I judged directors in direct proportion to how useful they were to me, how useful they seemed to be to other actors. I had no prejudices against them at all.

SLIDE: In 1941 you also made *H. M. Pulham, Esq.* for King Vidor. Did you think he was a better director than Mitchell Leisen?

BROWN: Oh much. Perceptive and deeper. King Vidor was a much better director. And I had a better role—quite a good role—in that film.

SLIDE: Did you socialize at all with the Hollywood community?

BROWN: No. My social life was the Lab. My total life was the Lab. I was earning my money, and I just went over there to do it, and came back, like you do if you work in a law office.

SLIDE: The other thing that happened in 1941 was that you married Ginny.

BROWN: We met at Stanford. She had been involved in theatre. When I went off to New York and had my other girls, she wanted to marry me very badly, but I didn't want to get married. I resisted marriage completely—right to the end. She went and taught school in the San Joaquin Valley. I came back out here. We lived together for a while and, eventually, went off to New York together. Finally, my mother sent a telegram: "Don't send me a Christmas gift this year. Just marry that nice girl you're living with." I thought it was quite reasonable for a Quaker mother to have waited that long, and so I did marry her.

SLIDE: Your first major role was in *Calling Dr. Gillespie* in 1942.

BROWN: Yes, I guess so.

SLIDE: That was the first Dr. Kildare film without Lew Ayres.

BROWN: Yes, but it was made with Lew Ayres. It was part of the Kildare series, and we made it, and I played "the case" around which the whole thing centered. As a result, I was to be under contract to Metro because it was a good role and they liked me. The film was just about to be released when Lew Ayres was called up for the draft and decided to be a conscientious objector. Metro got scared to death. They couldn't release this film with a conscientious objector. Nobody would come to see it. Just at that time, I was called into the army. I was down at Fort McArthur, waiting to be shipped to some training camp. They got me out, which Metro could do very easily, for an additional four weeks. We reshot all the stuff that had both Lew Ayres and me in it, replacing Ayres with Philip Dorn. They couldn't call the series Kildare anymore, so they called it Gillespie, after Lionel Barrymore. It was wonderful for me. I got out of the army, and I made some more money.

SLIDE: You were only in the army for a year?

BROWN: A year and a half. It robbed me of my M-G-M contract. I was to have been under contract to M-G-M when the army put me under contract. They picked up the option first. When I came out, Metro wasn't interested. They took Van Johnson, and he took over the roles I would have played at Metro. So they had no use for me when I came out.

SLIDE: The director of *Calling Dr. Gillespie* is Harold Bucquet. Is that pronounced "bouquet"?

BROWN: Bouquet. Harold Bucquet was, well if you could say Metro ever made "B" pictures, which they wouldn't say—low-budget films—he directed them. A real hack director. He just directed the camera, and changed it from here to here to here. A little bit of telling you what to do, and that was the end of it. Not a director at all—like many Hollywood directors.

SLIDE: How important was it to have a director who communicated with you? For example, I am told that Mervyn LeRoy, with whom you worked, did not direct actors.

BROWN: He was terrible. It's comforting to have somebody out there behind the camera, watching you, and to look in their faces when you've finished a take, and they say, "That's good." You can see from the eyes of the other human being whether you're making any kind of impression, whether you seem to be delivering what they want or think they want. It's terribly important, I think. My own approach to direction is that the director has one function, and one function alone, and that is to lure the performance out of the actor. If I'm directing you, I can't paste the performance on you because you're the guy who's doing it. I can see what I see in you as a human being and as an actor, and see what I can help you to illuminate, to draw out of you, but I can't paste it on. That's my view of being a director.

SLIDE: You would argue, therefore, that a director does not need to understand the technicalities of filmmaking. The most important thing is to understand his actors.

BROWN: I think so. For instance, when I did start to direct, I was very fortunate to have a good cameraman. I asked for a lot of help. I had been on the other side of the camera. I knew what films were about. I needed an enormous amount of help, and I always sought it. What the hell, they know where to put the camera, the best angles, whether it should move or not. Why should I have to know about that? I know the actors and what they should be doing, what I want from them.

SLIDE: As an actor coming from the theatre, did you find it difficult not shooting in sequence?

BROWN: Yes. It was tough. But you soon adjust to it. It's not insurmountable.

SLIDE: Tell me about Mervyn LeRoy.

BROWN: A shit, the worst shit in the whole world. Mervyn LeRoy was the kind of man who likes to have a whipping boy on any given production. I was it on that film with Claudette Colbert, *Without Reservations* (1946). I was the whipping boy. He cost RKO an awful lot of money because of me. He would say I cost RKO an awful lot of money. This is a failing of mine, I must say, that I learn the lines in a play or in a film by learning what I am talking about, not by learning the exact lines. I had an easy time learning the lines of *The Glass Menagerie*, which were good lines. I was on stage two and a half hours out of three, talking all the time. Easy to learn! Simple dialogue I never could learn. The reason I got into trouble with Mervyn LeRoy was that I was supposed to have known every "if," "but," and comma; and if I didn't, he made me do it over again. That flustered me. He embarrassed me in front of everyone, which I thought was terrible. That was no way to get a performance out of me. If he really was terribly concerned, he should have taken me aside and talked to me. But he didn't. He wanted to be a dictator. He was a dictator. I don't want to remember what the man looks like. I really hate him. Never worked with him again, wouldn't have worked with him again.

SLIDE: A director who has a cult reputation is Reginald LeBorg. I get the impression that he was a hack.

BROWN: He was a real hack. He just had the advantage of being terribly European, and having an accent. I know he's a cult. I was absolutely amazed when I read in recent years articles in some esoteric London newspapers of a Reginald

LeBorg festival. I nearly fell off my chair! The pictures he made were just crap. They really were. Of course, in Hollywood, they just adore the European accent and the European manner and the European gestures, and all that. And that was what Reginald LeBorg traded on.

SLIDE: Was he a nice guy?

BROWN: Oh, he was all right. He was just a nice faker, that's all. Technically, I think he knew what he was doing, how to work with a camera.

SLIDE: A couple of films you made in the late 1940s were major films noir, *The Killers* [1946], directed by Robert Siodmak, and *Johnny O'Clock* [1947], directed by Robert Rossen. Were you aware of the term "film noir"?

BROWN: No. I don't remember *Johnny O'Clock* at all. I'd forgotten I was even in that film. They were just films. I was never a great film buff. I was not very discerning about it. They were just films, and either I liked them to see or I didn't like them to see. I either enjoyed playing in them or I didn't. I felt they were either worthwhile or not worthwhile.

SLIDE: Do you recall anything of the directorial technique of Robert Siodmak?

BROWN: He was very clever with the camera.

SLIDE: It's interesting how you jump about from one film to another totally different. While you were doing these films, you made *If You Knew Susie* [1948] with Eddie Cantor, and *The Luck of the Irish* [1948], directed by Henry Koster.

BROWN: [laughs] Eddie Cantor was just fun to work with. He was a funny man. I don't remember Henry Koster at all.

SLIDE: At this time, were you selecting your parts, or did you just take anything you were offered?

BROWN: Oh, I always took everything the agent got me. Because I wanted the money to get back to the Lab. I just wanted to earn some money.

SLIDE: How did it come about that you went to England to play in *The Glass Menagerie*?

BROWN: When *The Glass Menagerie* was first played on Broadway, it was bought by a famous actor-director called Eddie Dowling. He directed it and cast himself in the role of Tom, which was crazy because he was thirty-eight or forty years old. Tennessee Williams had actually wanted me to play the role then. I had known Tennessee very slightly at Smithtown, during the last summer of the Group Theatre. Molly Day Thatcher, Elia Kazan's wife, was the play leader, in charge of scripts for the Group, and she was always seeking out young, talented writers she wanted to bring along—and Tennessee was one of them. He really felt I was right for this role, but I couldn't do it because Eddie Dowling bought it. When the play was to be done in London, and Helen Hayes was taking over the play, Tennessee talked to [producer] "Binkie" Beaumont in London and said, "There's a guy who originally should have played this role. Bring him over." So I went. It was just sheer luck. I didn't know Tennessee well at all, but he seemed to think I was the right guy for the part.

SLIDE: Helen Hayes had no control over who was to play opposite her?

BROWN: I think she probably accepted what Tennessee said.

SLIDE: I always have a problem appreciating Helen Hayes. On screen, her performances are generally mediocre, and she comes across as an irritating old lady.

BROWN: She was.

SLIDE: Was she a great actress?

BROWN: No. I don't think so. She was a skilled technician of the very old school, but she was very wrong casting for *The Glass Menagerie*. It was originally played by Laurette Taylor. Yes, she was of the old school—and she was a terrible drunk too. Laurette Taylor was what that woman should be, lousy and vague. Helen Hayes was precise, like a little sparrow. And she could not be anything but that. I thought she was wrong for it. In fact, that was a very difficult experience for me. John Gielgud was not a great director for her. I don't think Gielgud was a great director. John was a marvelous actor, but, believe it or not, he does not know how to deal with actors. He didn't know how to deal with Helen. I was in a tough position because I had directed some plays in the Lab and Helen knew I was a director. She used to take me aside and ask me to talk to her. Jesus Christ! Me talk to her, and she's being directed by one of the most famous actor-directors in the world. I couldn't do it. First of all, I wouldn't do it. I wasn't the director. He was the director, and whatever was to be done, it was his responsibility. So I had to skirt around her, and it was painful. There were a lot of things I wanted to tell her, but I just couldn't. I kept my discipline, and it was discipline to keep my mouth shut.

SLIDE: Was Gielgud in awe of Helen Hayes?

BROWN: No, Gielgud was not in awe of anybody. He just did not know how to handle her at all.

SLIDE: Do you think it might be also because he was English, and this was a very American play?

BROWN: Yes, I think it was a mistake to have Gielgud direct it in the first place. I just don't think he understood. You see, I think that is the difference between directors in England and directors in America. The directors in England don't get as deep into plays as American directors do. American directors dig deep into the psyche of people, the backgrounds, the social backgrounds, and so forth. We arrived, Helen and I, on the *Queen Mary*. We were invited to Binkie's lunch to meet Gielgud. We came to the theatre and read the play. John said, "Thank you very much, see you tomorrow." Now, in the Group Theatre, Harold Clurman would have talked about that play and the background for three days before you opened the book. John Gielgud says, "Mr. Brown, you will stand there," and they're off and running.

SLIDE: There was no talk of motivation?

BROWN: Nothing, absolutely nothing. That was a shock to me, but I'm self-sufficient as an actor. I had been acting for some time and I had been directing, and I just rolled with the punches and played the part.

SLIDE: At that time, had you considered staying in England?

BROWN: No, I hadn't considered staying in England. I stayed because I was offered a job in *Obsession* [1948, released in the United States as *The Hidden Room*]. We were sort of on our way home when this job came up, and I took it because it was good, a leading role.

SLIDE: Tell me about the director, Edward Dmytryk.

BROWN: Well, I was surprised to find that Eddie was on the board of the Lab from time to time. He must have been one of those guys who was put on the board of directors just because he was famous. I don't remember him being at any of the meetings. I was a big meeting-goer. I thought it was my duty to be there. Anyway, I knew him slightly. I knew his position politically, and I admired his standing up to the UnAmerican

Activities Committee. I did not admire him as a director. He didn't have much to say to actors. He was an arrogant little man. Oh boy, what an arrogant little man he was! It was a good role, an interesting role, and Bobby [Robert] Newton was fun to work with when he was sober.

SLIDE: It was not a major film?

BROWN: No. It's a good thriller. And Eddie did know how to use a camera—very much so. I just didn't like him.

SLIDE: Even before what happened later?

BROWN: Even before he became a shit. There are some people in this world you like, and some people you don't like. I just found him arrogant and not particularly warm and friendly as a director. Then, when I was just about to come back to America, he brought up the idea of my working with him on *Give Us This Day* [1949]. I was offered at that moment another job playing with Cornel Wilde in a film to be made in Switzerland for which I was to get ten thousand dollars. Wonderful! In any case, I decided to work with Dmytryk. I was to be his assistant and maybe play a little role. I didn't look forward to being his assistant, but if I ever fell in love with a film script on paper, it was *Give Us This Day*. I just felt it was the best film script I'd ever seen in my life. So I decided to forgo the ten thousand dollars, which was a stupid thing to do, in order to work on *Give Us This Day*. I think it's a good film, and I think Dmytryk directed it very well.

SLIDE: Apart from his personality, what was the problem in being Dmytryk's assistant?

BROWN: I just didn't like him. And an interesting playback on that is that when Dmytryk confessed and came out of jail, he along with Richard Collins became the experts to whom anybody would go who wanted to find out about somebody else. When I went to confront the American Legion, who were thumping me when I came back here, I said, "How do you know I'm a Communist?" And they said, "Well, we talked to two guys, and they said you'd been very cool to them." I said, "Who said I was cool to them?" I finally got it out of them: Eddie Dmytryk and Richard Collins. Now the interesting thing is that I had not seen Dick Collins for twenty-five years. So how could I be cool to him? Eddie Dmytryk, when I came back here, I would cross the street if I saw him coming. So how could I be cool to him? That's bullshit. That's the position the stool pigeons have to take. If somebody comes to them and says, "Is this man a Red?" They say, "He's not been very nice to me," because they've decided you've been a bad boy. It's part of the game.

SLIDE: You came back to the United States to direct *The Harlem Globetrotters*?

BROWN: To go back a little bit, when I finished *Give Us This Day* in England, I wasn't quite sure what I was going to do. About that time, Max Arnon sent me a cable and offered me a job as a dialogue director under contract to Columbia, leading to be a director. He had a film with Margaret Sullavan [*No Sad Songs for Me*, 1950], and the director was Rudy Mate, who had been, up to that time, a good cameraman. Rudy wanted to be a director very badly, and Sullavan was a very big star, who wasn't very happy with this cameraman being her director. She wanted somebody to talk to her about the acting. So Max Arnon brought me back to England to work specifically with her. It was fun, and I enjoyed it very much. I hated being a dialogue director, but I enjoyed working with her. That's how I came to be at Columbia, and I did dialogue directing on some real crap there. Eventually, Sidney Buchman had this script, written by his nephew, Alfred Palca, a sports writer from New York, on the Harlem Globetrotters. It was not a good script at all. Sidney Buchman, who was, after all, left wing and knew something about me and the Actors' Lab, thought I would be a good man to work with these nonactors—these black ballplayers—and make actors out of them. It was my first and only directorial job in the studio back here.

SLIDE: Did you ever pause and consider that this was a black film and that it should have a black director?

BROWN: Not at all. Nobody thought about it. There weren't any black directors. I just thought myself fortunate to get any job as a director and to be working with Sidney Buchman. In the end, it wasn't Sidney Buchman, you know. It was too small a picture for Sidney to do, so Harry Cohn got Buddy Adler in to do it. Buddy Adler had been in the shorts department at Metro, and this was his chance to move up—and, oh boy, Buddy was a mover. Buddy had nothing to do with the picture—nothing! It was Harry Cohn's habit to show the pictures on Tuesday night in the projection room at Columbia. Everybody at the studio bloody well had to come because he had spies and knew whether everyone had been there. Two pictures were shown: Bob Rossen's *Brave Bulls* and mine. The Globetrotters film came first and people rather enjoyed it. It was a cheap "B" picture, but it was fun and it was unusual. Next came *Brave Bulls*, which everybody hated. The next day, Buddy Adler called me into his office. Do you know what he looked like? He looked like the devil—a very handsome, gray-haired, solid-ironed face. He said, "Now look, Phil, I want you to understand something—I discovered you." I thought, Hell, he didn't discover me at all. Now that the picture was a big success, he said, "I don't want you ever to forget that I discovered you."

SLIDE: What was happening with the Actors' Lab by this time? How long did it last?

BROWN: It gradually grew from 1941, and finished about 1951. I was one of the members of the board of directors the whole time, never missed a meeting. Talk, talk, talk, all the time.

SLIDE: How did it end?

BROWN: It ended because it was attacked by the California UnAmerican Activities Committee, called the [State Senator Jack B.] Tenney Committee. That sort of put paid to it.

SLIDE: Did the members flee the Lab when they discovered they were under investigation, or did they stand together?

BROWN: They stood together at the time of the Tenney Committee. That whole thing is a little bit vague to me for the simple reason that I was in England for a year and a half, and during that year and a half, '48, '49, the Lab was beginning to fall apart. The Tenney Committee was held before I left. I didn't appear before it. I was at the hearings, but I was not called. Various people on the board of directors were called and had to speak.

SLIDE: When the House UnAmerican Activities Committee and the Tenney Committee began their work, were you aware just how horrific the outcome would be?

BROWN: It looked for a time as though the industry was going to stand up to those bastards—and they could have. But they just caved in and behaved like we should have expected them to. Individuals had no defense, and the group of ten couldn't win without the industry.

SLIDE: How did you react to fellow actors, such as Robert Taylor and Adolphe Menjou, giving evidence on behalf of the right wing?

BROWN: I despised them and I thought they were fools.

SLIDE: How would you have reacted, after Adolphe Menjou gave evidence, if your agent had called and offered you a role in his next film?

BROWN: I think I probably would have done it. Oh sure.

SLIDE: Did you think the right wing had as much right to its opinions as the left wing?

BROWN: Of course they did. To me, the whole concept, the whole premise on which it was based, that the Communist Party was going to take over America, was going to take over the picture business, was just dumb, just pure, unadulterated horseshit from the beginning. A lot of people thought the Lab was dominated by Communists, and there were a lot of Communists there. But if the Lab was dominated by Communists, it meant that the board of directors met in secret before they came into the Lab to meet. And if they did, there was precious little unity, because all of them had different opinions that they shared at the board meetings, every single one of them. They couldn't have taken over the house next door, let alone Hollywood, let alone the U.S. Government. That was pure bullshit.

SLIDE: There was no secrecy that someone like John Howard Lawson was a Communist?

BROWN: I certainly thought he was. Ninety percent of my friends, I think, were Communists. I could name them, but I won't—ever.

SLIDE: If you had been called before the committee, how would you have reacted?

BROWN: The same as they did. I just would have told them it was none of their business. I was not a member of the Communist Party.

SLIDE: But would you have said you were not a member?

BROWN: I would have said, I will not answer that question. I don't think it's your business to ask me that question. That's what I think I would have said.

SLIDE: In the early 1950s, you directed some Schlitz Beer programs for television.

BROWN: That was after the door was closed to me. I knew

by this time that I was on the way out. What happened was Columbia offered me several pictures to direct that I felt were such crap. I wasn't going to do them. I can only guess, but I think they were offering them to get rid of me. I bid good-bye to Sidney Buchman and left. I didn't think I'd ever get another job, but by this time I had taken on a new agent, Otto Preminger's brother, a wonderful man, a clever, clever man, who bucked the blacklist. He took me on and got me a job with Eddie Lewis, who was just beginning in the television industry. He had the backing to make an anthology series of twelve shows. He got different writers to write each half-hour segment and he had them released through the Schlitz Brewing Company. He got minor stars—Ann Harding, Edmund O'Brien—to star in each of these, and the theory was that each could be extended into a series. There were hundreds and hundreds of pilots floating around Hollywood, and he got twelve pilots for free. He also signed up Irene Dunne to be the mistress of ceremonies. I directed three—Jane Wyatt was in one, Edmund O'Brien in another, and Bobby Driscoll in the third. I managed to get through seventy-five or a hundred setups a day, with a three-day shooting schedule. Incredible!

The man who wrote one of the films was Luther Davis, a very good screenwriter. He said, "You can't have Irene Dunne just sit in a chair. Let's make her act." So, he devised an opening in which Irene Dunne, wearing a nice evening gown, came through a door in a large room and walked toward the camera. The camera tracked with her, and she passed a whole lot of strange props, as if she were walking through a room where props were stored. Then she passed by a pillar, disappeared, and when she came out the other side, she might be dressed in a football costume, because this was going to be a film about football. Then she did a funny little one-minute sketch, in which she acted and introduced what was coming. Eddie took me on to direct Irene Dunne. I had worked with Irene in *Over 21* [1945], so I knew her slightly. At first, she didn't want to do it. Eddie, Luther, and I went out to her house, took the scripts along, and she said, "Oh boys, I can't do this." We said, "Of course you can; give it a chance." And it was just wonderful. She responded to me! She did them all in two days. She'd never worked so hard her whole life. She said to me, "Phil, you're going to direct my next picture." That's the end of the story. When the shit hit the fan, I was finished with Eddie Lewis. The American Legion attacked me. Roy Brewer [the head of the union IATSE in Hollywood and a fervent anti-Communist] attacked me. I thought I would see how Irene Dunne would respond to this. I called her on the telephone, and I got a maid who said, "Who's calling please?" She came back and said, "I'm terribly sorry, but Miss Dunne is engaged and can't speak to you." She never did. She was very, very right wing. The shit really hit the fan. I won't go into all that. It's long and boring. Then, all of a sudden, I got a cable from Binkie Beaumont, saying Paul Scofield was in a play called *The River Line* by Charles Morgan—Paul used to play Americans occasionally—and he wanted to move on to something else. Would I like to come and take over? Would I like to! He sent me the script and I just hated it, but I got on the first boat I could get on. And I was out of the States for twenty years.

SLIDE: There was no problem in your getting work in the United Kingdom?

BROWN: Two things: First, I was already a name, and second, British Equity was known to be very nice about people who were blacklisted. The secretary of British Equity was, I think, a Communist, and Laurence Olivier, the president, was very liberal. It was also a reasonable idea. I wasn't taking a job away from a British actor. There weren't many British actors who could play Americans. That would help me in the future, because when I was finished with *The River Line*, I was supposed to get out of the country, but I stayed and another role came along.

SLIDE: So you were typecast as an American in England on stage and film?

BROWN: I didn't do much film work there. For years I was in the theatre. I played *Sabrina Fair, Teahouse of the August Moon, The Caine Mutiny, The Tender Trap*. They were all leading roles. I worked in the theatre constantly, and was working in television for Doug Fairbanks [Jr.]. He had an operation going, making television shows for America.

SLIDE: How did the relationship with Fairbanks come about?

BROWN: While I was playing in *The River Line* in 1952,

Fairbanks was just starting to do his television series for American consumption. They were half-hour shows, an anthology series, and I played one or two leading roles. He rolled out the red carpet for me, saying, "The Madison Avenue boys say they can't understand British accents, so they want to put in as many Americans as possible." I was being paid very well for it. All of a sudden, one Sunday, I got a telephone call from Fairbanks's assistant, a big, tall, handsome guards-officer type, who said, "Will you come over and have a drink with me?" So I went to his house, and he showed me a telegram from Roy Brewer in California. The telegram said, "Dear Mr. Fairbanks, If you use Phil Brown in any more of your films, I will see to it that your contract is cancelled." I had a meeting with Doug, and he felt terrible about it. . . but said, "We can't use you anymore. Your name will have to be taken off these things." I said, "In exchange for taking my name off, the next time your business people from America come here, I'd like to talk to them." A few months went by, and he called. His backer, Elliott Hyman, a big financier, was coming over. In the office were Doug Fairbanks—who wanted to be called Sir Douglas although he couldn't—his assistant, and little Phil Brown. We faced two guys, Elliott Hyman and his aide, who looked and talked just like American gangsters out of a Hollywood "B" picture. It was just so corny. We began to talk in general, and soon Doug Fairbanks and his assistant faded out the door. Here was little Phil Brown facing these two gangsters with their cigars. Hyman said, "Now look, Brown, you're in trouble, but we can get you out of this." I played it very naive and said, "How can you do that?" He said, "It's easy. There's a man in America called Martin Gang. He knows a lot of FBI agents. They'll look you up, they'll write up a statement for you and you just say if this is true or not." They must have been stupid to think I didn't know this was a scam. I said, "Really, and how much will this cost me." They said, "Not much. About five hundred dollars." I said, "I'm insulted. I have heard that people like Fredric March and John Huston each had to pay about ten thousand. I may be a sucker. I know I'm not that valuable. But five hundred is insulting. In the second place, I won't do it, because they'll ask me to sign something that I won't sign. I came here to this meeting with you, having told

Douglas Fairbanks I would tell you anything you want to know. But I'm not having some bastard in New York look up my past, confront me with it, and make me sign something." That was the end of the meeting. I just walked out.

SLIDE: And you never worked for Fairbanks again?

BROWN: Oddly enough, I did. About six months later, out of the blue, he called me up, and I did two more of his series.

SLIDE: It was never suggested that you should work as a production assistant or director on the series?

BROWN: No. I wouldn't have. I was an actor, and that was that. You see Roy Brewer was one of my main adversaries here.

SLIDE: Are you suggesting that Roy Brewer had it in for you specifically?

BROWN: He sure did! At the time Adlai Stevenson was running for president, he was coming to Los Angeles to address a big meeting here. Roy Brewer was on the Democratic Committee for Stevenson. Stevenson had made quite a principled, albeit politically stupid, speech in New York, decrying the American Legion's position as red-baiters. Have to go back a little bit . . . There was a director who used to direct the *I Love Lucy Shows* named Marc Daniels, who lived just up the canyon from me. He came to me and said, "We're going to make a television short for the Stevenson Committee. Want to be in it?" I said, "Sure." He said, "There's an undecided Republican and a Democrat in an elevator. They get stuck between floors. The undecided Republican is talked into voting for Stevenson by the Democrat, and they go on up and he's one of them. Do you want to play the Democrat?" I said, "Of course. Send me the script." The script didn't arrive, and finally I called him up. He started to stammer. I said, "You don't need to say, but I can tell you why. It's Roy Brewer, isn't it?" He said, "Well, yes, as a matter of fact it is." I said, "I want to meet Mr. Brewer. I have nothing to hide from him. I want to tell him everything there is to tell him." He said, "I'll see if I can arrange it." I called him again. No dice. By now I was mad. And I can get very mad. I've got a very bad temper. There was a man who was also on this committee named Philip Dunne, who was a very famous writer-director-producer. I didn't know him socially, but I had worked with him on a film, so I called him up. I said, "Look Phil, I know Mr. Brewer is preventing me from working on a film for someone who is my candidate just as much as he is his. I think this is quite terrible. How is it that a man on your committee can blackball another Democrat?" He said, "Don't worry about it. You'll meet him." I called again and again, and he said, "Mr. Brewer won't meet you because he understands you bring along a lawyer." I said, "Well tell Mr. Brewer he can bring along his lawyer. I don't give a Goddam." He refused to meet me. So I hit upon a plan. I composed a five-hundred-word telegram to Phil Dunne, saying I thought it was utterly ridiculous that a man like Roy Brewer should be supporting a candidate who had just got through damning red-baiters in Washington. Phil Dunne said, "Please don't send it. Don't rock the boat. I'll arrange for you to meet Stevenson." Stevenson came and went. I tried to get in touch with Phil Dunne after that. Just like Irene Dunne, he wouldn't talk to me. Phil Dunne claimed to be a smoother-over, supposedly one of the people who helped people get off the blacklist. Well, he really wasn't.

SLIDE: Philip Dunne was a typical Hollywood liberal?

BROWN: Oh he was! He was a terrrible phoney. I've read in his book [*Take Two*, McGraw-Hill, 1980] that he excuses the fact he left Roy Brewer on the committee. He uses the phoney old Hollywood writer excuse about a whore with a heart of gold. Enough of Phil Dunne!

SLIDE: I was going to ask you about some of the films you made in Britain. George Moore O'Ferrall directed you in *The Green Scarf* [1954].

BROWN: A charming man, a real charmer, very relaxed, laid back, upper class. A good director.

SLIDE: You lived opposite the film's leading man, Michael Redgrave.

BROWN: They had a big house just diagonally across from our houseboat. We bought our first houseboat, a Canadian motor torpedo boat from the First World War, which was sunk, in the early 1950s. Then we bought an empty steel boat.

SLIDE: Redgrave's bisexuality was commonly known?

BROWN: I think so. I do know it was a source of problems in the family. He had a chauffeur who was his boyfriend living in the house with him and Rachel [Kempson, his wife].

SLIDE: What about *The Bedford Incident* [1965], directed by James B. Harris?

BROWN: That was an American film. He was a nobody. Richard Widmark was the star, and Widmark was really the director. Harris was just there to do what he was told.

SLIDE: *The Adding Machine* [1969], directed by Jerry Epstein?

BROWN: Jerome Epstein was one of Chaplin's boys, a terrible pain in the ass. The word "obsequious" was invented for Jerry Epstein, the most obsequious human being I have ever seen in my life. He was just terrible. I had known him slightly in Hollywood because he used to run a theatre here. He was not a director at all. He was just an ass kisser.

SLIDE: You appeared in *Operation Cross Eagles* [1969], directed by and starring Richard Conte.

BROWN: It was directed by a Yugoslav actually, but Conte took credit. It was a tiny little Yugoslavian film, one of those usual things about the Americans showing the Yugoslavs how to win the war. America's always showing everybody how to win the war. This was Conte showing the Yugoslavs how to win the war.

SLIDE: When did you first move to Yugoslavia?

BROWN: When we were supposed to do a film called *The Boy Cried Murder* [1966]. That was the remake of a Bobby Driscoll film called *The Window*. I was to play the father, and a little English boy played the boy. Neither Ginny nor I had been to Yugoslavia, so instead of just flying out, we took my car and my fourteen-foot catamaran. And we fell in love with the place. Ginny learned to speak Serbo-Coatian. We went back the next year, and we stayed a whole year. Then we went back again and again to an island off the coast of Croatia, every year for twenty-five years. We did it partly for economic reasons. You could live in Yugoslavia for nothing.

SLIDE: While you were there, did you continue to work in films shot in Yugoslavia?

BROWN: Occasionally I would get a job. I was basically an actor—always in English. They were all little things. Kirk Douglas's *Scalawag* [1973] was the only assistant director thing I did.

SLIDE: Were your last films *Star Wars* and *Superman* (1978)?

BROWN: *Superman* was nothing. I had a reasonably good role in *Star Wars*. I can say to some young person I was in *Star Wars*, and they say, "Gee!" If I told them I was in *H. M. Pulham*,

Esq., they'd ask what that was all about. That's a far more important film than *Star Wars*. It's ironic.

SLIDE: Did you voluntarily retire from films?

BROWN: I sort of moved away from it. The idea of working in a film now absolutely terrifies me.

SLIDE: What were your best performances on screen?

BROWN: I suppose *Obsession*, the Dr. Gillespie one, and, oddly enough, *H. M. Pulham, Esq.*

SLIDE: Do you wish the blacklist had never happened, or do you think it made you stronger from a moral and ethical viewpoint?

BROWN: No, I wish it had never happened. The only reason I wish it had never happened is that I was just getting off the ground here as a director. When I came to Britain, I couldn't work as a director because British films were controlled by American money. Jules Dassin had lots of friends, so when he went to Europe, he could work. So could Carl Foreman and Joe Losey. It was a big battle for me. I like to think that had I stayed in Hollywood, I might have been an important director. I might have turned out to be another hack. But that's enough of that!

ROSE HOBART

Bette Davis may have had a popular song named in honor of her eyes, but Rose Hobart is quite possibly the only actress to be the title of a film. Rose Hobart has enjoyed starring careers on both the stage and screen, and yet she may well go down in history as the title of a classic avant-garde short by artist and filmmaker Joseph Cornell. That film captures one aspect of Rose Hobart—her luminescent beauty as it fascinated Cornell in the 1931 Universal horror film *East of Borneo*. It ignores the ability of Rose Hobart to enhance any film no matter how second-rate (and she did appear in a great number of minor films). Reviewing *East of Borneo* in the *New York Times*, Mordaunt Hall wrote, "Miss Hobart serves this picture in her usual intelligent fashion," and that phrase might well serve, in turn, to describe much of Rose Hobart's work on screen.

Born in New York on May 1, 1906, Rose Hobart was the daughter of the then well-known musician Paul Kefer. She made her stage debut on the Chautauqua circuit in the late teens, becoming a major Broadway actress in the 1920s. Miss Hobart made her New York stage debut in *Lullaby* at the Knickerbocker Theatre on September 17, 1923; she appeared as Charmian in the 1925 Theatre Guild production of *Caesar and Cleopatra*, was cast in the title role of Eva Le Gallienne's classic production of *Alice in Wonderland* but had to leave the cast through illness, toured opposite Noel Coward in *The Vortex* (1926), played opposite Helen Hayes in *What Every Woman Knows* (1926), and made her London stage debut in *The Comic Artist* at the Strand Theatre in 1928. As a result of her performance as Grazia (played in the screen version inadequately by Evelyn Venable) in *Death Takes a Holiday* (1929), Rose Hobart was invited to Hollywood, where she made her screen debut in *Liliom* (1930).

Under contract to Universal, Rose Hobart starred in *A Lady Surrenders* (1930), *East of Borneo* (1931), *Compromised* (1931), and

Dr. Jekyll and Mr. Hyde (1932). The last gave cinematographer Karl Struss a unique opportunity to capture on celluloid Rose Hobart's screen radiance—she is badly photographed in *Liliom*, and the lighting gives her an oddly harsh and at times almost evil appearance. Of course the role of Dr. Jekyll's sweetheart, Muriel Carew, is an intrinsically dull one, but Rose Hobart overcomes the basic lackluster coldness of the character in the one major love scene in the garden with Fredric March. The fireworks may belong to Miriam Hopkins, but the sureness of a finished actress is evident from Miss Hobart's performance.

Joseph Cornell utilized footage from *East of Borneo* for his first collage film, *Rose Hobart* (also known as *Tristes Tropiques*), in the late 1930s, and critic P. Adams Sitney has described the work as representing "the intersection of his [Cornell's] involvement with collage and his love of the cinema."

Rose Hobart returned to the stage in the early 1930s and could be seen in *I Loved You Wednesday* (1932), *Girls in Uniform* (1932), *Springtime for Henry* (1933), and *The Wind and the Rain* (1934), among others. Her last major stage appearance was as Cynthia Randolph in *Dear Octopus* (1939). The actress returned to the screen that same year, not as a star but as a featured player in films such as *Susan and God* (1940), *Lady Be Good* (1941), *Mr. and Mrs. North* (1941), *Conflict* (1945), *The Farmer's Daughter* (1947), and *Cass Timberlane* (1947). She also starred in a couple of "B" pictures, *Prison Girls* (1942) and *The Soul of a Monster* (1944), and the twelve-chapter serial, *The Adventures of Smilin' Jack* (1943).

With *Bride of Vengeance* (1949), Rose Hobart's screen career ended, not through any fault of her own, but rather because she was named by the House UnAmerican Activities Committee and was, for all intents and purposes, blacklisted. Once she angrily told an interviewer, "I've been accused of being everything from a Communist to a lesbian, but I was only interested in making things better for people." Rose Hobart did not make a third return to the screen, but she did appear in a number of television series from the late 1950s onwards.

An intelligent and attractive personality, who can be considerably outspoken, Rose Hobart has lived in retirement at the Motion Picture Country House and Hospital for a number of years. In 1994, Scarecrow Press published her autobiography, *A Steady Digression to a Fixed Point*.

ANTHONY SLIDE: Both your parents were involved in music, so why did you decide to go on the stage?

ROSE HOBART: Father was first cellist for the New York Symphony, first violinist for the Metropolitan, and he had a quartet up in Woodstock, New York, where we spent our summers. I started learning ballet up there. Once, when I was about six, Edna St. Vincent Millay came up because they were doing her play, *Aria da Capo*, at the festival. She was living next door to us, and I haunted her. We used to sit in a daisy field between the two houses and talk about the play. Her sister was playing the lead, and it was at that time that I decided I wanted to be an actress.

SLIDE: Did you train?

HOBART: No, I didn't. A man called Percival Vivian, who had come here from England with the Ben Greet Players, was living with his wife on Long Island. Things were not good at home, and we were sent to stay with them for a couple of weeks. At that time he was directing shows for Chautauqua, and I was busily acting out these parts because the scripts were lying about the house. Three days before they were to leave for New Orleans, which was the first stop on their tour, the ingenue quit. Percy was frantic, and his wife said, "Why don't you listen to Rose?" He did, and three days later, I was on a tour of one-night stands through Louisiana, Texas, and Arizona, and ended up in Billings, Montana.

SLIDE: Of the plays in which you appeared in the 1920s, which do you consider the most important?

HOBART: The only really good one was *Death Takes a Holiday*, which was what brought me out here to pictures. I was tested by both Fox and Universal. I knew the play was closing in June, and I wanted to stay with it, 'til it closed. Universal agreed to that, and so I signed with them. Then, the next day, Fox said, "But we've already assigned you a picture!" The picture was *Liliom*, in which I had done my first legitimate acting on tour with Joseph Schildkraut and Eva Le Gallienne. So I wanted to do *Liliom*, and I said I would come out and do that ahead of my contract with Universal. I was given the big treatment at Fox because they knew they didn't have me for very long, but when I went over to Universal they treated me like a dog.

SLIDE: Was the transition to films very difficult?

HOBART: I was very lucky because I really didn't know what the difference was, and I had Frank Borzage as a director. He was just great. He was the one who said to me, "What you feel doesn't matter a damn on film; it's what you're thinking. That is what will register." I thought he was only used to picture actors who don't know how to act. So we came to the death scene in *Liliom*, and he said, "Do you want to rehearse it?" And I said, "No, I think I know how to deal with it." This was nine o'clock in the morning—a fine time to have to emote. We shot it thirty-five times—a very big head close-up. Finally he said, "Print the eighteenth and thirty-second take." And I said, "Will you do me a favor and print the first one!" Because during the first take, I was crying my eyes out and giving a "performance." I went into the projection room the next morning, and they threw this thing on the screen. And after the first five minutes it was ludicrous. It was just awful. Because the face never changed, the expression didn't change. I was crying real tears and it was awful. And the eighteenth take, where I'm talking to myself, just like an actor, was great. I said thank you, because nothing else would have convinced me that emotion doesn't register on the screen.

SLIDE: How do you feel about *Liliom*? Were you pleased with it?

HOBART: Not really, because Charles Farrell was so awful. Of course, he did it to me the very first day. He was playing his ukulele, and he came up to me and said, "You New Yorkers are so sophisticated; how do you get that way?" in his high, squeaky voice. I thought to myself, he's kidding. But he wasn't. When I saw *Liliom* in New York, I was coming into the lobby, and I said, "Hey, Charlie doesn't sound too bad." But it turned out it was me talking on the screen.

SLIDE: It is a very stylized film. Were you aware of that at the time.

HOBART: No, I wasn't. I was so horrified with what they did with the sets—after the theatre. The play that Ferenc Molnar wrote was about a poor little honky-tonk guy and a serving girl, and the room they lived in was a hovel on the outskirts of

Budapest. In the film they have this great, immense place. To me, it took away from the whole thing. Again, when he died in the play, he went to the only place he could picture, which was a third-rate police station. He would not be able to imagine anything else because he'd never known anything else.

SLIDE: It's strange, considering you were under contract to Universal, that you made only two films at the studio.

HOBART: Because, unfortunately, the first one I made was *East of Borneo*. That did it! Working with animals and working all night almost killed me. I was fighting with the management all the time because they didn't care. They only cared about celluloid that you can sell. What you do on the celluloid they didn't care about.

SLIDE: But thanks to *East of Borneo* we have Joseph Cornell's *Rose Hobart*.

HOBART: Yes, but I only hope *East of Borneo* isn't in existence any more, because it was the schlockiest film ever made. The whole thing was phony. The sets were phony. The characters were phony. And I was miserable because Charles Bickford, my leading man, and I didn't get along. We fought like roped steers through the whole picture. The last night he almost killed me when we were filming the sequence in which we run out from that awful castle place. We started out, and I suddenly realized he was going to slam me up against the wall at the end. I thought, I'm going to get it now! The crew apparently noticed, because they made a flying wedge and let only him through, blocking me. He wasn't expecting that and ran flat into the wall, banging his head. Of course, I couldn't leave well enough alone and said, "Better take care, Bickford, or next time you'll break your damn neck." Right after that, they said, "Will Mr. Bickford and Miss Hobart please go to the stills department to photograph the love scenes."

SLIDE: Your next major film was *Dr. Jekyll and Mr. Hyde.*

HOBART: That was a loan-out. Almost everything I did was a loan-out from Universal. It was easy to work with Rouben Mamoulian because he liked me and knew I was a theatre actress. *On East of Borneo* I was working with George Melford, who was an old silent director. In those days we had dialogue directors, and he'd let the dialogue director and me decide how we were to play a scene. Then we'd shoot it. Melford would wait until I'd finished talking, cut the sound, and direct me by talking me through the scene over again as if it were a silent picture. I did every scene twice.

SLIDE: About this time you returned to the stage?

HOBART: I had a big dramatic argument with Junior Laemmle, and Universal said of course they would let me go, because they didn't want anyone who wasn't happy. I wanted to go back to New York because I'd started having analysis before I came out here and I wanted to get back and finish that up. Out here, I felt like something without its shell. I was too vulnerable.

SLIDE: You returned to the stage for the remainder of the decade, but why, then, did you decide to return to the screen?

HOBART: Because I wasn't getting the parts I wanted. Everyone who had been successful in films was coming back to the stage, like Maggie Sullavan, and getting the plum parts on Broadway. I thought, Oh shit, now's the time to go back and make it again. And on top of that I was getting a divorce from my husband, and I thought this was a good excuse to take off for the coast.

SLIDE: And you went back to Universal for *Tower of London* (1939).

HOBART: Yes, but, thankfully, it was no longer Junior Laemmle's Universal.

SLIDE: For the next ten years you played supporting or featured roles.

HOBART: What I was doing was playing leads in the "B"s and supporting roles in the "A"s. I was freelancing. I'd had my fill of being a contract player.

SLIDE: Which films offered you the best parts during this period?

HOBART: I suppose *Susan and God* and *Claudia and David* (1946). I don't have any recollection of liking any of them particularly. When it's not your show, if the part is good, you do the best you can in it.

SLIDE: You were not concerned you were being typecast in horror films such as *The Mad Ghoul* [1943], *The Soul of a Monster* [1944], and *The Cat Creeps* [1946]?

HOBART: No. I was doing other things in between. As a matter of fact, I missed one I was supposed to be in with

Karloff, *Isle of the Dead* [1945]. He got sick after we'd shot all of the long shots, and by the time he came back, I was working on another picture and they had to replace me. But they left in all the long shots of me, and I can recognize myself.

SLIDE: You worked with a lot of directors we never hear about these days, men like Willis Goldbeck, Robert Sinclair, James Hogan, Will Jason, and S. Sylvan Simon. Do you have any remembrances of them?

HOBART: I don't remember any of them. They were just totally unimportant as far as I was concerned. By that time I was established as a good second woman, and they just let me play it the way I wanted to.

SLIDE: Your career in films ended when you were blacklisted. How did that come about?

HOBART: I was doing a play called *The Male Animal* for the USO, in which I played the lead. Ellen Corby was in it; she played the maid, and that was her first acting job. The play was produced by the Actors' Lab, and that was what started my being blacklisted—because I was a member of the Actors' Lab. When I returned from a USO tour of the Aleutians with the play, I walked back into the strike at Warner Bros. I was hearing both sides, and none of it made any sense. So I went over to Warners to see what was going on, and I happened to get there just as the guards started using the water hoses on people. I was horrified! I thought, you can't do this to actors! (I don't know why I think we're special.) Finally, I got called up before the House UnAmerican Activities Committee because of being a board member of Actors' Lab. I read a prepared statement in which I very carefully said nobody could push me around. At that time I was doing a play called *Deep Are the Roots*, and that didn't help either because it was about what they now would call miscegenation. Anyway, when that was over, I suddenly found I wasn't acting anymore.

SLIDE: When did you learn that you were to be called before the committee?

HOBART: I was never warned about it. Gradually, people were taken. Five of us from the Actors' Lab were finally tapped. We had to go.

SLIDE: This was February 19, 1948, in Los Angeles.

HOBART: Yeah.

SLIDE: This may be a stupid question, but why did you refuse to answer the question?

HOBART: Because there were several members of the Actors' Lab who were Communist members. We didn't want them to get harmed, so we decided that we would all have to do the same thing. We refused to answer as a group.

SLIDE: Did you know there would be repercussions, or did you think nothing more would happen?

HOBART: Oh, no, no, no. You see it was a little late. We were the last ones they talked to. We were the last of the Mohicans. So we knew exactly what was going to happen.

SLIDE: Were you married at the time?

HOBART: Yeah.

SLIDE: Did your husband agree with your actions?

HOBART: Yes, he did. He disapproved of what they were doing. Thank God! He was a good Republican, and before I went before the committee, he got a lawyer to go with me. And the lawyer was a Republican. He was horrified at the things we went through. I think I convinced him that this was ridiculous, this was something that should not be happening. I felt like saying I had made a Christian out of him.

SLIDE: What about your agent?

HOBART: I didn't have an agent.

SLIDE: Did you feel that your career was winding down?

HOBART: It was beginning to wind down when it happened. Then it got worse and worse. I knew I was dead then.

SLIDE: You didn't shed any tears?

HOBART: No, because so many people were being attacked. I was just one of the group.

SLIDE: I have a copy here of your entry in *Red Channels*. Let me ask you whether you remember the organizations, etc., in which it is claimed you were involved. Progressive Citizens of America?

HOBART: Yes. That was just a group of people who disapproved of what was going on at the moment. Why they conned me into it, I'll never know, except at the time I was fairly well known in the theatre. I was a name.

SLIDE: We know you were a member of the board of directors of the Actors' Lab.

HOBART: Yeah.

·SLIDE: You were also, apparently, one of the sponsors of the Scientific and Cultural Conference for World Peace.

HOBART: Believe me, half of these things I never knew.

SLIDE: So you've never heard of this?

HOBART: No.

SLIDE: You were a sponsor in Mexico City of the American Continental Congress for World Peace.

HOBART: No, I was not. I never went to Mexico City. One of the fascinating things was that I got accused of everything that went on in Mexico, and I hadn't been to Mexico at that point.

SLIDE: You signed a petition to the Supreme Court asking for a review of the convictions of John Howard Lawson and Dalton Trumbo.

HOBART: Yeah.

SLIDE: Did a lot of people sign that petition?

HOBART: I don't know how many did. I felt very strongly that it should be written, so I signed it. And by that time I was dead anyway, and I knew it. The other thing was to be like the guy who got me into it, the one who put the finger on me, an actor I had worked with at the Lab.

SLIDE: Who was that?

HOBART: I know his name as well as my own, but I can't remember it when I want to [Lee J. Cobb]. I resent it because he said he had been in my house at a meeting of the Communist Party, where I was present. A bloody lie! I called him and said, "I want to talk to you." It turned out that he knew damned well that I hadn't been there, because I hadn't. What he said was, "I never would have mentioned you had they not brought it up." I thought, how stupid can you be. Obviously, they would con people into telling things. He said it had been January or February, and, sure enough, I was in the Aleutians. And I could prove it! I had all of that material, which I took eventually to the committee. I said, "Look, kids, you say I was here in my house because some silly shit says I was." It didn't make any difference.

SLIDE: You tried to clear yourself?

HOBART: Yeah. The lawyer my husband had gotten had been an FBI guy. He said, "Request a passport. If they don't want to give you a passport, call me and we'll fight it out." So I did, and I got my passport. So I thought, okay, now I'm free.

But nobody ever knew. It was too late anyway.

SLIDE: *Red Channels* and other publications were the work of Myron C. Fagan. Were you aware of him?

HOBART: Oh sure. *Red Channels* was the worst one. Almost everything in it was a lie. Never met Fagan. Never saw him. Never knew who he was. If you're blacklisted, it's not going to do any good to nail the person who blacklisted you. That's only going to make it worse.

SLIDE: Why couldn't you have sued Fagan for libel?

HOBART: I could have done it, but my husband said no. Let it lie.

SLIDE: You must have felt bitter at the time.

HOBART: Oh yes. People avoided you. They went across the street. I thought, Oh shit, there goes another one. I was always asking, what have I done that you think was so awful that you're not going to speak to me anymore. Nobody would say, wait a minute, let's just look into this and see what the hell this is all about. The minute things get rough in the theatre and film industry, you get kicked out.

SLIDE: Did your son Judd come along later?

HOBART: Judd saved my life. I had him practically two days after I had the conversation with them [the committee]. I had somebody to look after and somebody to look after me. I knew damned well I wouldn't be working again.

SLIDE: I think you've revealed something scandalous today in that your husband was a Republican.

HOBART: To me he was ridiculous being a Republican. But he turned out so well over this, he won me over!

SLIDE: Eventually you returned to work in television.

HOBART: I decided to go back to work when my son was in his teens, and Ruth Birch, a casting director, got me a part on *The Danny Thomas Show* on television. Finally, I became a semi-regular on *Peyton Place*.

SLIDE: How do you feel about nostalgia?

HOBART: I'm not much for nostalgia. I think I was in the best era of pictures both times: the first time when talkies were just coming in, and then in the 1940s. The town is now run by bankers and businessmen who don't give a shit about the theatre or movies the way the original guys did. This was started by guys who had a dream.

MARSHA HUNT

An intelligent and attractive actress, whose youthful charm and personality tended to camouflage the level of her versatility on screen, Marsha Hunt was a featured player or leading lady in some sixty-two Hollywood productions released between 1935 and 1972. Born in Chicago on October 17, 1917, Marsha Hunt grew up in New York, graduating from the Horace Mann School for Girls at the age of sixteen. Immediately she began to pursue an acting career, studying at the Theodora Irvine Studio for the Theatre and working as a model with the John Powers Agency.

At the age of seventeen, in June 1935, Miss Hunt signed a contract with Paramount, making her screen debut in *The Virginia Judge* (1935). She made twelve films at Paramount, including *The Accusing Finger* (1936), *Easy to Take* (1936), and *Murder Goes to College* (1937), together with two loan-outs at 20th Century-Fox and RKO. When Paramount failed to renew her contract, the actress became a freelance performer, initially working at Republic and Monogram before returning to the major studios for *These Glamor Girls* (1939), *Joe and Ethel Turp Call on the President* (1939), *Pride and Prejudice* (1940), and *Cheers for Miss Bishop* (1941), among others.

In 1941, Marsha Hunt began the happiest years of her film career as a contract leading lady with M-G-M, beginning with *The Penalty* (1941). Among her other M-G-M productions are *Blossoms in the Dust* (1941), *Panama Hattie* (1942), *The Human Comedy* (1943), and *A Letter for Evie* (1946). She ended the contract with a loan-out to Universal for *Smash-Up, The Story of a Woman* (1947). The following year, Marsha Hunt made her Broadway debut in *Joy to the World*, directed by Jules Dassin.

On March 6, 1950, Marsha Hunt was featured on the cover of *Life* magazine. At the same time, she was also experiencing the effects of the blacklist. Although never called before the House

UnAmerican Activities Committee, Marsha Hunt is prominently featured in *Red Channels*. Her "crimes" according to that publication were that she signed a petition to the Supreme Court, asking for a review of the convictions of John Howard Lawson and Dalton Trumbo; she spoke, by recording, at a rally organized by the Stop Censorship Committee, held at New York's Hotel Astor on March 23, 1948; she signed a statement in 1946 issued by the Hollywood Independent Citizens Committee of the Arts, Sciences, and Professions; she was a speaker at a rally held in Los Angeles on October 16, 1947, by the Progressive Citizens of America; she was a member of the Committee for the First Amendment; and she signed a statement protesting the House UnAmerican Activities Committee. By mutual agreement, Miss Hunt and I avoided discussion of the blacklist. "I'm disinclined to have any more attention called to that painful time as it affected me," she explained. Our interview took place at her home in Sherman Oaks, California, where she has lived since 1946.

ANTHONY SLIDE: How would you describe your family background?

MARSHA HUNT: Idyllic. I don't know that I've ever met anyone who could say that, or does say it, but I lucked into the most fortuitous, warm, constructive kind of family context imaginable. My father was a top scholar, a Phi Beta Kappa. My mother was a voice coach and accompanist of singers in the concert and opera fields. We didn't have the term "liberated woman," but my mother certainly was. She wasn't militant—well, maybe faintly so. My sister and I—I had a sibling a year and a half older—never once felt neglected because of the demands on her time. My parents met in the choir loft of a church. She was the organist and he the new choir director. Mother was the daughter of a Baptist preacher, and my father was a Methodist. We were brought up Methodist, not because of any great strong feeling in my parents, but because the nearest church was a Methodist church. They were brought up, both, in the state of Indiana, which is now called the Bible Belt. They were wholesome, they neither smoked nor drank, and they never used the Lord's name in vain. I never heard a four-letter word. It didn't exist in my wholesome family setting.

SLIDE: When did you decide you wanted to be an actress?

HUNT: I think at the age of three or four. I was taken to my first stage production—I think it was Gilbert and Sullivan's *HMS Pinafore*—and I came home entranced and remained that way for life. There is this dreary story of my mother coming upstairs and finding her bedroom door closed. She came in to see what was happening, and I was seated in front of the three-way mirror on her dressing table, crying my eyes out uncontrollably. She rushed to comfort me, and I said, "Go away, I'm acting." Apparently, I was acting for my own benefit with these three-way mirrors, just enchanted by the sight of tears.

SLIDE: You wanted to be a stage actress initially?

HUNT: Well, that's all I knew about at that age. I guess I later saw Charlie Chaplin and Harold Lloyd and all those others, but I remember Mary Pickford and, of course, Douglas Fairbanks. At some point I became movie struck, not stagestruck. I was going to be an actress in movies. The only way I can account for that is I saw a lot more movies than plays. They were more affordable. They were closer to where we lived. The Broadway theatre was saved for birthdays and Christmas and special treats.

SLIDE: You selected the name Marsha?

HUNT: My birth certificate says M-A-R-C-I-A Virginia Hunt. I didn't know this until I was, I think, fifteen. Mother and I sat in a darkened theatre, watching a Joan Crawford movie in which she played a character named Marcia, spelled the old, legitimate, English way. Mother leaned over in the dark and whispered, "That's your real name." That was the first time I had heard the name Marcia. I was Betty Hunt. Nothing wrong with Betty. It just sounds terrible with Hunt. It's staccato. There's no flow. There's no legato to it. You sort of spit it out. Anything was preferable to Betty, and I thought Marcia was a very pretty name. I right away tried it out on my chums at school. Nobody had heard the name, and they said, "How do you spell it?" When I spelled it for them, they said, "Oh, Mar-see-a." And I said, "I don't think it's like that—it's Marsha." And I determined sometime around then that if ever I had a chance to have a professional name, it was going to be spelled so there was only one way to pronounce it. It all came to pass, and I did enter films as Marsha Hunt. I suppose I coined that spelling of the name, which is now, I think, in more common usage than the original.

SLIDE: Did your parents encourage you to go to Theodora Irvine's Studio for the Theatre?

HUNT: You have done your research! They were very disappointed when I chose not to go to college, which both of them had done. The reason I didn't was that we couldn't locate a single college or university in the land where you could major in drama before your third year. Not having been able to find one, I decided what to do instead. I finished school at sixteen, having skipped a couple of times in the early years. I custom made a preparation for an acting career in films. I became a model to learn about the visuals of lights, camera, makeup, grooming, and whether or not I photographed. For the auditory, because talkies were in now, I went to a series of auditions at NBC downtown, trying out for their radio dramatic staff. They had a roster, a vocal stock company. Toward the end of my first year out of school, I had a call from NBC to say I had finally passed and they were putting me on the "available for casting" list. I had to say, "I'm packing as we speak to go west."

SLIDE: How did Paramount find out about you?

HUNT: I called myself to their attention. This was the brainchild of two photographers, Robert and Sarah Mack, for whom I'd done a lot of ads. But when I was sixteen, just out of school and starting to model, they had a hunch about me. It's such a long story! Gabriel Pascal was newly arrived in this country, with a reputation only in Europe, and the Macks wanted me to meet Gaby, as they called him. He was a scary-looking man. He glowered, never smiled. He had a gold tooth that shone enchantingly, and when he finally did smile, the sun came out. It was beatific. But, with his thick Hungarian accent, he was terrifying to this young girl. He had me prepare a scene from *Romeo and Juliet*. His Romeo was memorable, I must tell you! After we read the scene together, he informed me I was going to be greater than anybody. He had me lie down on the floor with books on my stomach so I could learn to use my diaphragm and speak with some force. It was ridiculous but, yes, he decided I was to have a career.

SLIDE: I'm surprised that Pascal had the power to persuade Paramount to give you a contract.

HUNT: He didn't. He decided I must study at London's

Royal Academy. That was "the only decent preparation for the English-speaking stage." We right away wrote to the Royal Academy, who right away wrote back, "We're full up; try us next year." So I had to kill a year. Gaby undertook to select for me where I should go, and he settled on Theodora Irvine's Studio for the Theatre.

SLIDE: Was it a well-known establishment at the time?

HUNT: I couldn't tell you. Happily, she was only a couple of blocks from where I lived, 73rd Street, just off Riverside Drive, on the West Side. She was a sorority sister of my mother's, and, this being the Depression, we needed a partial scholarship, which she granted. She was a grand old lady of the theatre. What her career had been, I don't know. But before the year was out, I was under contract to Paramount. The way that happened was that the Macks left New York and moved to Los Angeles, where they opened a public relations firm, publicizing movie people. By chance, they met this great-uncle of mine, and they conspired. The Macks decided that Hollywood was really quite childlike, and they thought maybe child psychology would work. If you forbade a child to eat something, that's what the child would scream the house down to be allowed to get to eat. "We are going to tell Hollywood about you, and then we're going to tell Hollywood it can't have you, and see what happens." They brought me out here, with uncle bankrolling everything. They took some pictures of me in Peter Lorre's garden—he was a client of theirs—and the pictures were planted. It must have been the quietest news day of the year, because I broke page one, section two, of the *Los Angeles Times*, and four wire services carried the story, "Model Spurns Films." The reporters said I was New York's number one model. Well, I was miles from being New York's number one model. I worked part-time as a model. I hadn't been on any magazine covers. But nobody knew that I hadn't. They all rushed to say, "And you're going to be in films, Miss Hunt?" And I said, "Oh heavens, no." The Macks wanted me to say it was the furthest thing from my mind, but I was brought up to tell the truth. So I shaded it. I didn't make an outright lie. Instead, I said, "Well, in fact, I do want to be an actress, but I don't think I'm ready. I plan to go to London and study at the Royal Academy." It was the man-bites-dog story because, of course, models wanted to be in the movies, and this one didn't. That was all it took. Four major studios offered me a screen test. They found me an agent, who was Zeppo Marx, and he chose the best of the offers, which turned out to be Paramount. I made a test for Paramount, which was taken very seriously. They spent three weeks preparing this test. I didn't just sit in front of the camera and babble on about myself. I did three different scenes, two from *Morning Glory* and one from Noel Coward. They were directed by Phyllis Lawton, who later became the elected mayor of Beverly Hills and the wife of George Seaton, a fine screenwriter. She didn't direct feature films. She was the head of the talent department. She directed my test obviously very well, because Paramount was so excited about the result that they exercised the option. I was paid at the outset more than people like Betty Grable and Ann Sheridan, who were under stock contract to Paramount at maybe seventy-five dollars a week. I was paid two hundred fifty dollars a week, which would be at least twenty-five hundred dollars today.

SLIDE: How many years was the contract for?

HUNT: Seven years. All contracts ran a potential seven years. The first year or two had six-month options—the studio's option, not mine. After which it was every year, and each time with a rise in salary. So I was Paramount's new find no less.

SLIDE: Your first film was *The Virginia Judge* with Walter Kelly.

HUNT: Within weeks of taking up the option, they put me right to work. The first time I got paid to act was in a major studio feature film, a film probably shown all around the world. What a scary way to learn your craft. In front of everybody. I've no idea how good or bad I was, but they kept putting me in romantic leads.

SLIDE: The star of the film, Walter Kelly, had a pretty racist act in vaudeville. Was the film racist?

HUNT: Stepin Fetchit was in it. And all I can tell you is that there was a scene at a fair or carnival at which one tried one's skill at hitting a target with, I think it was, a baseball. The target was Stepin Fetchit's head. It made me ill that anyone's head could be split open. It just made me sick. I don't know that I thought of it as cruelty to blacks, but to anyone. I complained and, of course, it had no effect. I guess the audience found it screamingly funny. Stepin Fetchit was such a dear man, so sweet, and so good at what he did, which was not Uncle Tomism, but playing a very slow human being.

SLIDE: Was it a characterization, or was he slow in real life?

HUNT: He was intelligent, certainly far more intelligent than the roles he played. The scratching of the head, the "yes, ma'am"—that was a characterization. He was certainly not stupid. He memorized his lines. He got laughs. There was some skill to what he did.

SLIDE: You followed *The Virginia Judge* with a couple of Westerns.

HUNT: A total of four. The second picture was a loan-out to 20th Century-Fox called *Gentle Julia* [1936], and that was a screen version of a Booth Tarkington novel. I was Julia, the title role, but actually the star of the picture was Jane Withers, who was the brat character, 20th's balance to Shirley Temple. After *Gentle Julia*, then I think came the Westerns.

SLIDE: It seems a retrograde step, a bad career move, to appear in a Western. Did it bother you?

HUNT: Well, I had no choice. I don't remember if I thought it was a backward move or whether I simply didn't fancy Westerns because I had seen so few and the ones I had seen were such formula stories. The girl, the love interest, was a device of the writer with very little to recommend her as a human being, as a person of any dimension. I do remember complaining to the front office that I was not sure what I was doing in a Western. I should be in an Eastern. I was from New York! Not that I wanted to be typecast, but I didn't feel I was an outdoor type. I remember the answer, "Marsha, you're a tall girl, and you're going to look tall in the saddle against the skyline."

SLIDE: Did you learn to ride?

HUNT: I had learned to ride at summer camp in Maine, but they asked if I could ride. They said, "How do you ride?" I said, "Not terribly well." And they said, "We don't mean how well. Do you ride English or Western?" They said I rode English, and I had to unlearn. I think I had four sessions before we started shooting. I enjoyed the Westerns. They were harsh in that there were no restrooms. You were way out, miles from anywhere, and I remember thinking I would burst the first couple of days.

I was so tender and unsophisticated; it didn't occur to me to go to the assistant director and say, "Where do I go? What do I do?" I just suffered and contained and contained, until, finally, I found the tallest shrub possible—and there weren't many.

SLIDE: You are an intellectual, being given scripts that you often must have looked at and thought were awful.

HUNT: Again and again.

SLIDE: What was your mind-set? Did you feel you had to do them to build a career, or did you fight and try to get better roles?

HUNT: A little of both, I guess. It's quite true, you did as told. And I was brought up an obedient child. I obeyed an order. That was the discipline that I understood. Also, I was earning my spurs. I realized that I was extraordinarily lucky to have been given the start that I had in the career of my choice. I was starting at the top, the feminine lead. I did no bits, no walk-ons, not even supporting featured roles. The fact that the material was pretty pedestrian was distressing to me. My dream was drawing-room comedy. I had a knack for comedy. I appreciated it, and I was dying to play it. I suppose I thought I was getting my basic training toward what I was best suited to, and what I wanted most to do. I only complained mildly. For one thing, Paramount had a different boss almost every week or month. We had so many different bosses that you hardly knew who was on first base. Ernst Lubitsch was the head of the studio at one crazy point, and he knew nothing of administration. It was not my nature to rebel. I simply did the best I knew how with what I was given to do. Whether I was growing in the process, I'm not in the position to judge. I did feel at Paramount that everything they gave me was somewhat similar to all the others, with only a change of wardrobe, a change of title, or a change of leading man. But it was pretty much the same formula.

SLIDE: Among the directors you worked with at this time are Robert Florey, Frank Tuttle, and Mitchell Leisen. What was different in their techniques?

HUNT: That's not an easy thing to answer. The directors—very few of them directed very much. Florey—yes. That was a good role [in *Hollywood Boulevard*, 1936] of those twelve I did for Paramount. It was an emotional role and had some lively moments with Bob Cummings as leading man. I just remember enjoying Florey and being very comfortable with him. I can't tell you any anecdote or be specific about it.

SLIDE: Frank Tuttle was more political.

HUNT: Was he?

SLIDE: Were you aware of his liberal stance?

HUNT: No. Nothing was happening in 1936, which was when I think we did *College Holiday* [1936]. That was, of course, Jack Benny, George Burns, Gracie Allen, Martha Raye, Ben Blue—fabulous, wonderful vaudevillians and comedians. I played the love interest, Jack Benny's daughter.

SLIDE: A thankless role in a film like that.

HUNT: I think so. I don't remember much about it except I got to sing two songs. I played opposite Leif Erickson, who had a beautiful baritone voice, and we sang to each other on a dance floor, in a tree, and in a gondola. Frank Tuttle was fun, owlish. I enjoyed him. I had very little of his attention. He was trying to keep track of some wide-open comics who were one-upping each other. We went on location to Santa Barbara, and we stayed at the Santa Barbara Biltmore, which was very staid and very upper crust. And our cast having dinner in the dining room! Butter and spitballs and rolls were being hurled through the air, and Martha Raye was in full cry. It was kind of a circus. I had a lovely time. Now Mitch Leisen was one of my goals. I dreamed of working with Mitchell Leisen. And I can't really say that I did. *Easy Living* [1937] is listed as a film that I'm in because I was given screen credit. That film starts with a mink coat falling out of a penthouse window in New York and landing on Jean Arthur. That was the cute beginning that launched the whole light comedy. At the end of the story, that same mink coat is tossed or falls out of an upper-story window and lands on me. It was their conceit that it would be fun to have it fall on a familiar face rather than an extra. I don't think I spoke a word. I don't know how long the camera was on me walking down the street before I was obscured by the mink coat. But that's it. It's a screen credit that's a joke. I never worked for Mitch Leisen. If only I might have worked for him! I saw everything that he directed that I could because I thought he was the best at that kind of sophisticated comedy direction.

SLIDE: Were you disappointed that Paramount did not renew your contract?

HUNT: Mixed feelings. It was a blow to be dropped, to become a has-been at the age of twenty. On the other hand, I felt it had become a blind alley leading nowhere. What I used to do was to sneak a look at the script of something Paramount was starting to schedule for production, find a role that had some color, some body to it, a challenge, and then go to the producer or the front office and plead for that role. They'd say, "But that's not the lead." And I was never allowed these. They thought I was ungrateful for the leading roles they gave me. In fact, if I'm not mistaken, I sat out the third year. I made those twelve pictures in the first two years, and the third year, I didn't work. I think the last thing I did for Paramount was another loan-out—to RKO. It was a terrible picture set in Annapolis [*Annapolis Salute*, 1937]. Again, the feminine lead, "the girl," with a bunch of leading men, Jimmy Ellison, Van Heflin, and Arthur Lake. I had no chance to show Paramount what was in me to play. So it was a relief to that extent, but I was facing a bleak and uncertain future.

SLIDE: Of course, after leaving Paramount, you worked at one or two very minor studios.

HUNT: Poverty Row!

SLIDE: Was that a mistake or a challenge? Did your agent tell you to go and do it?

HUNT: No. Your agent was to seek and find you work. Then you as a client had the right to turn it down or accept it. I can't tell you much about my frame of mind except that I wanted to work. Maybe I felt financially that I had to work, because I had not grown rich at Paramount. I married in '38.

SLIDE: He was the head of the editing department at Paramount?

HUNT: The assistant head. Jerry Hopper was his name, and I nicknamed him Jay. When we met, Jay was the assistant head of the music department. Boris Morros, the head of the music department, didn't do much administering. He was a colorful character, very entertaining, but Jay really did the work. He was making thirty-five dollars a week when I first met him, and went up to forty-five dollars by the time we married.

SLIDE: How did he feel knowing his wife was making so much more? Was this a problem?

HUNT: I now understand. I think subconsciously then that it

was. But he was so gallant, so gentle, and so polite. He never articulated that. It must have been a test of his maturity. He was almost ten years my senior. He never complained, never divulged any embarrassment or sense of humiliation about it. He understood the studio system well enough to know that the people working in other departments were making tiny fractions of what actors were paid. Jay was awfully good about it, but I know it must have eaten at him. We married in November '38, and I left Paramount during June of '38. Already in the fall, I was working for Poverty Row. The first picture I did was *Come on Leathernecks* [1938] for Republic, with Richard Cromwell as leading man and Leon Ames as heavy.

SLIDE: Was working at a Poverty Row studio very different from working at Paramount?

HUNT: Yes. Schedule. We completed a feature film in six days. If a plane didn't go by overhead and spoil the sound-track, they printed it. No second or third take. If you approximated the script and no props were broken—print it, next setup. It was breathtaking, a challenge. It was tremendous discipline. You didn't just learn your lines, you knew what you were going to play that day as the person you were going to be. You had your performance ready because there was no direction. You were told what door to come through, where to sit, when to get up. You were told the physical moves, but the performance had to be yours, or there wasn't any.

SLIDE: Was there snobbery? If you had been in two Monogram films, would M-G-M be wary of casting you?

HUNT: Yes, there was a caste system of studios. M-G-M was the crown of moviemaking.

SLIDE: Your first film at M-G-M was one of the Andy Hardy films [*The Hardys Ride High*, 1938].

HUNT: One day's work.

SLIDE: When you went on the set, did the other actors look down on you because you had just been working on Poverty Row?

HUNT: No. I don't think they knew what I had done in the quickies. What they did know was my name and my face, because I probably had as much publicity in fan magazines as anybody going. I don't think there was a fan magazine in those three years at Paramount in which I did not appear. I was known not as a star but as a leading lady. And I confess, the reason I did the Andy Hardy one-day bit was that I was so lonely for the smell of a major studio. I just wanted to work on a major lot again. Just for my morale. And it was an interesting role, a spendthrift wife whose husband is suing her for divorce because he can't pay her bills. What I must tell you is that I fell in love with M-G-M. I was braced for treatment as a bit player. I lectured myself before I went there, "Put your ego in your pocket and take what comes." Instead, I found a canvas-back chair with Miss Hunt stenciled on it. Now, granted, that was going to be burned and another canvas strip for the back of the chair would replace it tomorrow. But somebody went to the trouble of doing that. And, if you please, I had a change room on the set with my name on the door. I was so touched, I almost wept. I was so moved and grateful that I have loved M-G-M ever since.

SLIDE: One of your films from this period is *Irene* [1940], in which the leading lady, Anna Neagle, is married to the director. Were you aware that because of the relationship she was always going to get the best shots?

HUNT: Exactly. One knew that going in. And, of course, *Irene* is the title of the film, and Irene, the character, is played by Anna Neagle. One knew she was going to be the focal figure of the film. I went in with no illusions about it. But it was an "A" picture, and, after my three quickies, I was happy to accept it. Also, I got to work with some lovely players who were wonderful folk—Billie Burke, May Robson, Alan Marshall, and Ray Milland. I saw *Irene* for the first time in half a century a few months ago, and I could hardly find me. I really dismissed that film as something I had scarcely been in, but in those days I was grateful for the work, grateful for anything I could get. Now *Winter Carnival* [1939], that was rather interesting.

SLIDE: Did you go to Dartmouth College to shoot it?

HUNT: If only! My first love was a Dartmouth student. I had a great romantic aura built up about Dartmouth and its Winter Carnival. No, we shot everything that we were in at the Goldwyn Studios. Walter Wanger [the film's producer] was a Dartmouth alumnus. He was an independent producer with very nearly the Samuel Goldwyn kind of stature, an educated filmmaker who made good films; and while I was at

Paramount, he sent for me. He gave me a script to read, saying, "You're awfully young for this, but would you read it and maybe come back and read a scene with me? I'm so intrigued by your work that I have a hunch about you." He told me I would play opposite Henry Fonda. I went home and went to pieces over this script. I wanted it so badly! It was called *The Moon's Our Home* [1936]. Margaret Sullavan would end up playing it, and quite rightly. But, of course, I wanted it desperately. It was what I felt I was best equipped to play, but he said, "No, I'm afraid you're just too young." Then later he hired me for the second lead in *Winter Carnival*. The script was to be written by F. Scott Fitzgerald, who never sobered up enough to write it. He may have had some stabs at it, but he never turned in a script. And Budd Schulberg wound up writing it and ghosting it. He did turn in a screenplay, and then wrote a best-selling novel [*The Disenchanted*, 1950] about all that. So that made it a special film for all those reasons.

In the summer of '39, I had not broken through this limping career status, and I had reconciled myself to going back east and starting all over. I was going to try for summer stock. I was a household name because I had done so many movies and been in so many fan magazines, and ladies were naming their babies this pretty new M-A-R-S-H-A name, but I was certainly no star. I thought maybe I could get work in summer stock in New England and get some stage experience. Just then, Paramount chartered a special private train to publicize Cecil B. DeMille's *Union Pacific*, with Irene Dunne and Randolph Scott, and a brand new actor named Robert Preston—a train they were sending across the country. I was asked to join the celebrity junket even though I was no longer with Paramount. I had already done a pleasant junket for Paramount. So when I was invited to be on this special train, I said, "Yes, so long as I don't have to return." I got off in New York and was with my agent, getting in touch with producers of summer stock theatres, when a call came from my agent in Hollywood saying there was a part, the kind I had been dreaming of and wanting so badly. It was at M-G-M. They would test me, but would not pay my way back to California. A costly gamble. Decision! I flew back, made the test, and got the part. It shifted all gears. I was from then on an actress, not an ingenue. It was *These*

Glamor Girls, my first suicide, my first neurotic role. It was with an all–young player cast. It was Lana Turner's first lead. And it changed everything for me. From then on, there were no two roles alike. From then on, I was in ecstasy.

SLIDE: Before moving on, can I ask if the train ride was the first time you met Cecil B. DeMille?

HUNT: He wasn't on the train, but I knew him socially. I thought he was charming, but an egomaniac. There were so many jokes around the lot about DeMille. Oh yes, his films made money, but the crew, the people who made films, I don't know that anyone thought of him as a great director, except of spectacles.

SLIDE: How did the M-G-M contract come about?

HUNT: I made either six or seven movies for M-G-M before they decided it might be cheaper to have me under contract. Fred Datig, who had been the head of casting at Paramount when I was signed, was by then the head of casting at M-G-M, and Fred somehow was always in my corner. Fred believed in me as talent. I don't know how he may have felt about my potential for stardom, but I wasn't interested in stardom. It wasn't the pinnacle I was after. I wanted to be a good actress. I just wanted to be stretched to the limit and to grow in the process, and so I was ecstatic at M-G-M.

SLIDE: Were you concerned about your billing?

HUNT: No. I think I probably should have been. I think my billing was sometimes several rungs below where it belonged in the context of a film, probably because other players' agents got there first and got it written into the contract. I know that my billing suffered, but I didn't. I remember Robert [Presnell, Jr.], my eventual second husband [they were married in 1946], asked me one day when we were getting to know each other, "Do you want to be the greatest actress in all the land?" That's the way he put it. I had to stop for a minute. I had never been asked that question. And I said, "No, I don't think so." He said, "Oh good, because it's not in your nature. You're too gentle. You're not ruthless. And to be the greatest actress in all the land, you must be willing to climb on other people's backs." He was relieved! I had never quite examined myself in those terms. It was the quality of work that I was after, not its prominence or its dominance. I wanted to excel myself. I wanted to be the best I possibly could. Now, mind you, I had no false modesty. I knew that I was greatly gifted. That's not a boast. It's a fact. And the word "gift" is literally that. It was what I was equipped with at birth from the Gods, from my parents, or who knows. What you do with your talent is another matter, is to your service or disservice. I was blessed six ways from Sunday, as they say. I could have done any number of things, and have done several things besides acting. I think that a career in movies and on the stage and television is in good part the expression of ego. You want to be noticed and recognized, you want to be praised, you want to hear applause, to get good reviews.

I was not interested in the Hollywood star-building system, because I think in those days, stardom was largely structured by distilling a personal quality and projecting one's own personality again and again in slight variations of the theme. Instead, I vanished into my roles, projecting as little of myself as possible from one role to another. They were vastly different, and so was I. Persons would come up to me and say, "That wasn't *you* I saw." And I'd be tickled that people couldn't connect me from one role to another. That early title I was given at Metro as "Hollywood's Youngest Character Actress" is the proudest thing I can record. I played four old ladies before I was thirty, a Brooklyn showgirl, society snob, schoolteacher, unmarried mother, army nurse, two nightclub singers, crime lab technician, spoiled heiress, symphony harpist, farm girl, and two suicides, among others.

SLIDE: How much lead time would there be from the point when you got the script to when you started shooting?

HUNT: Very often very little. Barely time to get your wardrobe fittings out of the way and, more recently, not even fittings—you went shopping.

SLIDE: How would you create a character?

HUNT: Almost entirely out of memory, your composite of a character. I've always been grateful that I grew up in New York because every day I rode the subway to school. You sat across from humanity in every shape and form, every age. I studied them all. When you went shopping on Fifth Avenue, you were exposed to other people, from other kinds of life, other backgrounds of opportunity and economy. I guess I used everybody

I clapped eyes on as someone to take from, to borrow from, to emulate. I think empathy is very important. If, in your nature, it comes naturally to you to put yourself in someone else's frame of mind, frame of emotion, then you know exactly how that person would respond, given this or that happening. I think most of it is imagination. Sense memory. Kitty, I think, was my character's name in *Joe and Ethel Turp Call on the President*, my first old lady. I was in my twenties when I played her, and I remember that I used two people as my example. One was an elderly housekeeper that we'd had, and the other was a great-aunt that I'd visited on her farm in Indiana. I was fascinated with older women's carriage, the way they sat, the way they worked their mouths, the way they squinted through their glasses. All these things were such fun for me to absorb and tuck away somewhere. I did not know an awful lot of elderly people, but enough to get me started toward playing Kitty.

SLIDE: Two of your first films at M-G-M were directed by Mervyn LeRoy, about whom I have not heard good things.

HUNT: Mervyn, in my experience, was not a director at all. He knew the mechanics of how to put a scene together. I can't remember a single directorial touch from Mervyn. I was fond of him—not terribly. He was not a warm personality. It was generally thought that Mervyn was getting by, by trading on an in-law relationship or whatever.

SLIDE: He did turn out some good films.

HUNT: I know. That's the script, the talent of the performers, the musical score. All those things. In *Blossoms in the Dust* he had Greer Garson and Walter Pidgeon, some good people to work with. We would run through our moves, and we'd get quiet on the set. And he'd say, "Now give me a nice scene, kids . . . Action!" "Give me a nice scene, kids"—it was like a little phonograph record he would play every time. And away we'd go in our own way. Perhaps Mervyn's gift was to stay out of the way of fine writing, acting, and camera work, trusting them to do their thing well.

SLIDE: You were the star of Fred Zinnemann's first feature film, *Kid Glove Killer* [1942].

HUNT: When I was given the script of *Kid Glove Killer*, I asked, "Who's going to direct it?" They said Fred Zinnemann. "Who's that?" I had never heard his name before. It was one of the best roles I'd been given—in a light comedy at last. I cared much about who was going to direct it. I didn't know what this tenderfoot would be like. The first day on the set—we never met before the first day's shooting—here was this small, slender, unimpressive-looking, delicate-looking man. He had the softest voice. You had to come close to make sure you caught what he was saying. Before we started anything, he asked everybody to come down off the catwalks and the structures, the distant members of the crew, everyone to come close. Then, speaking as loudly as he could, he introduced himself and he said, "You may have heard this is my very first feature picture. I think I'm prepared. I have worked toward this a long time. You, all of you, are good at what you do. I want to do my best. But, if any of you has a suggestion that would improve this product that we're about to create, I invite you to please come and tell me. I would like to consider it, and I would be grateful for your suggestions. Let all of us make the best film that we can." From that moment on, I think they would have died for him. No director had spoken with such humility, such openness and frankness. They adored him—as I did—from that moment on. I loved his direction. I loved the man. We became good friends. In fact, except for Jules Dassin, I got to know Fred better than any other director I worked for. I could have told anyone while we were shooting that picture that this man was destined to make fine films, probably great films. And indeed he did, over and over again.

SLIDE: When you were loaned out to Columbia for *None Shall Escape* [1944], were you given the script in advance of being told you would play the part?

HUNT: I don't remember the sequence of events. I just know that when I read it, I loved it, and was just so excited about doing something with that much emotion, that much current history. We were in the middle of the war with the outcome far from certain. And, so far as I know, it is the first film that showed atrocities against the Jews. Oh, no doubt about Hitler, that he was evil and had to be stopped. He was out to conquer the world. But his treatment of the Jews, I don't think that had reached the American screens yet. This was right there, with the shooting right in front of us of the rabbi as he was exhorting the Jews not to go like cattle into the cattle cars. And the

Nazis galloping their horses into the synagogue to use it as a stable. Wow! This was powerful stuff!

SLIDE: Did it affect you emotionally playing the part?

HUNT: All the time. I was deep into that character. I saw her struggle, because this was a man she had loved and she was prepared to marry and spend the rest of her life with. And he came back from the war a different person. Yes, he had a glass eye and a wooden leg, but that wasn't what stopped her. It was the change, the hatred—he was riddled with hate and bitterness. All of this I thought I understood. As to Bundy (Andre de Toth), I don't remember too many specifics about his direction, but it was excellent. It was an engrossing film. We got inside our characters.

SLIDE: With a film like that, how difficult is it to go home at night to your husband, become his wife and forget about the character you are playing?

HUNT: I think you take off the wardrobe and the wig and the makeup and the old-age and whatever, and you're yourself again. You come home and ask him what kind of a day he had. When I study the script for tomorrow's lines, then I'm absolutely into it again. In learning them and identifying how it's going to be tomorrow, you are back into that identity. It wasn't hard for me. I don't know how it is for other players.

SLIDE: Presumably, M-G-M just loaned you out and told you you were going to star in this film?

HUNT: Well, actually, at M-G-M you could get away with not doing an assigned role. I found that out because there was something or other I was assigned that I just hated. I said, "I don't want to do this thing; I'll take a suspension off salary sooner than play this." My agent quoted me as having said that to Benny Thau, who was the chillingly cold top executive under Louis B. Mayer. I was sent for and scolded for having mentioned the word "suspension" at M-G-M. M-G-M did not treat its players that way, and if I felt very strongly about it, of course I did not have to play the part.

SLIDE: You ended your M-G-M contract with a loan-out for *Smash-Up*, the Stuart Heisler film that made Susan Hayward a star. Were you aware that here was a special talent?

HUNT: I thought she was good, very good. I didn't feel she was great. I had seen her do good work before that and since.

I didn't know that was the star-making role, though it was certainly a meaty one. I'm not quite as fond of *Smash-Up* as television programmers seem to be. It's on TV repeatedly. Someone added that pretentious line, *The Story of a Woman*, as if there was something universal about that character. Better to call it *The Story of a Lush*. It's about a weak and self-pitying character, however appealingly Susan Hayward played her.

SLIDE: Your first film away from M-G-M is *Carnegie Hall* [1947].

HUNT: I was literally thrilled to play the central figure in a story that would bring together the top virtuoso musical talents of the world. My mother had played recitals in Little Carnegie, the recital hall adjacent to the concert hall, and I had attended memorable concerts there as I grew up. To be there was pretty wonderful, and back in New York, my home town—I'd been homesick for it all.

SLIDE: And the director was Edgar G. Ulmer.

HUNT: Yes, I had wondered who'd be chosen to direct a film of great music performed by great artists. When I was told the name, it was new to me. "Is he a musician?" I asked. And they said, "He plays a pretty good phonograph."

I'm afraid Edgar Ulmer was not my favorite director. Oh, he had the technique of film direction, but not the humanity. Always courteous, even deferential toward the soloists, the conductors, and me, he was often brusque and short-tempered with his crew and the supporting players. If only his gruffness had been consistent and impartial, I might have liked him better.

There was a scene I had with an elderly actor who probably needed the work. Somewhat nervous, he fumbled his lines a time or two. Edgar was quick with cutting sarcasm, which rattled the actor even more, and so he couldn't remember the words. Instead of bearing with or reassuring him, Edgar both ridiculed and berated him, until the old gentleman couldn't have told you his own name.

Near tears myself of sympathy for the player and outrage with the director, I walked away to my set dressing room and stayed 'til the assistant director came, asking, "Are you okay? We're waiting for you," and I asked to have a word with Mr. Ulmer. When he arrived, we had it out in my room. I said, I'm sorry I can't work with you if you treat people this way anymore. And until I have your word that you're going to treat players with dignity and enable them to perform what they're here to do, that's it. It was the only time I ever delivered an ultimatum. And it worked!

SLIDE: Could Ulmer have been in fear of you?

HUNT: Oh no, I'm sure not. But he probably was in fear of running behind schedule if I held up production over his treatment of people, so he obliged me, and was more controlled after that.

SLIDE: You came to the Broadway stage with *Joy to the World*, directed by Jules Dassin.

HUNT: I want to talk about him at M-G-M first. *The Affairs of Martha* [1942] remains probably the most fun of any film I've ever been in. It has a gorgeous cast. I didn't know who Jules Dassin was when we started, but by the end of the first day, I sure knew this was a man with a sense of comedy that was inspired. He was fun to be with. He was bright. He was New York. All kinds of good, comfortable things. He apparently had seen enough of my work to feel secure that I could deliver what he hoped for in the role, and we worked together hand in glove with utter joy. Then in 1945 we worked together again in *A Letter for Evie*, a World War II variation of the Cyrano theme with Hume Cronyn. I played an office-girl ingenue, and it was not challenging or comedically interesting, but working with Dassin was a delight.

In '47, I was shooting *Raw Deal* around the Goldwyn lot with Dennis O'Keefe, Claire Trevor, John Ireland, and Raymond Burr—a wonderful cast. We used to lunch together every day in the executive dining room, and one day I brought up my problem. I had been sent a script of a play to do on Broadway that I loved, but it was a starring role. What a scary way to break into live theatre with your name above the title on a marquee. Hadn't I better earn my spurs first, be a supporting player in something? "No," they said, "Go for it." And I said that what tempted me besides loving the script was Jules Dassin as director. They said, "You don't have any excuse not to do it." So, with their shoving and vote of confidence, I undertook it. There were other reasons. It was about the picture business, which I knew something about by that time. And the other reason was Alfred Drake, whom I had seen on Broadway in *Oklahoma*! The idea of being on stage with that kind of brilliance, that kind of dynamism, that kind of energy, was just too tempting to resist. I took the plunge and had beginner's luck.

SLIDE: Did you have to change your technique?

HUNT: I was conscious of projection of voice. There were no body mikes—there were no mikes of any kind—in those days. Your voice filled the theatre or you weren't doing your job. I didn't know if I could be heard, whether I had a big enough voice. I found out very quickly that I've got a big, big voice that carries well. The other thing was all the rest of me. I had almost never been shot, shown from head to toe. Nearly always it was torso, head and shoulders, or a close-up of just the head. And here were these great long things that went from my hips all the way down to the stage. What did I do with them? How did I stand? And my dangling arms! I kept begging Julie to give me a prop to hold. I didn't know what to do with my hands. He said, "Let them hang there." I don't know that I worried much about learning an entire role. What did scare me was drying up on stage, going blank. But didn't, happily.

There came the night—I think it was fairly early into the run on Broadway—when I came on stage, and suddenly, vividly, I felt the boards of the stage under the soles of my shoes. It was the darnedest sensation. I'm feeling the stage! I'm comfortable here. I belong here. And from then on, not that I had been nervous, but from then on, the stage and I have been the best of friends.

SLIDE: Is it fortuitous at this political time in American history that you were in New York, on the stage, rather than in Hollywood?

HUNT: Fortuitous? Well, actually, I think not. If I hadn't been in New York in 1950, and doing a great amount of radio and early television (then centered in New York), I wouldn't have been included in *Red Channels*, the far right-wing pamphlet that listed one hundred and fifty broadcast artists whom it considered of suspect loyalty because of left-wing political activity or association, and that hinted at their Communist Party membership or affiliation. At that point, fearful of product boycott and loss of customers, networks, sponsors, ad

agencies, and producers agreed to deem all one hundred and
fifty "unemployable." That actually began the blacklist practice, ending all our careers and livelihoods in broadcasting. I
don't know that the movie studios would have blacklisted me
if *Red Channels* hadn't named me and made them think I might
be a Communist. So to play safe, they put me on their secret
blacklist.

SLIDE: Did you know that would happen?

HUNT: No. Who could dream that? I didn't know the term
"blacklist." But even in the late 1940s, at Sardi's restaurant in
New York, I would see friends from Hollywood and they
would say, "Don't go back. It's getting awful there. Lines are
being drawn. People are no longer speaking to each other.
There's mounting suspicion, a mounting paranoia." I had not
experienced that except on the board of the Screen Actors
Guild in '46 and '47—as early as that—when they became obsessed with communism. I couldn't figure out why they found
that so fascinating. It had nothing to do with acting or actors'
working conditions. Yes, in October of '47, Robert [Presnell Jr.]
and I flew back with that protest planeload to witness the
Congressional hearings on Hollywood in Washington and to
try and put some sense of balance back before the public, to
assure them that it really was safe to go to the movies—that
they were not full of Communist propaganda. I think by 1950 it
was clear that the whole of show business was under political
siege. But, miraculously, the Broadway stage was spared.
People were not denied work on the Broadway stage. Movies,
radio, and television were overcome, but the theatre was not.
When I was unable to work in any of the blacklist media, I
could always do a play in stock, around the country.

SLIDE: In 1959 you appeared in *Blue Denim*, directed by
Philip Dunne. Was that out of friendship?

HUNT: I will never know. I can't think why else. You see,
nobody ever says they're recommending or hiring you because
you're blacklisted and they think that's wrong and it's an evil
thing.

SLIDE: Perhaps they're hiring you because you're talented?

HUNT: I always like to hope that might be at least an ingre-
dient. I would prefer it was the reason. I've never asked him,
how come I'm in your picture. Phil Dunne was one of nature's

noblemen. He was one of the three directors—along with John Huston and William Wyler—who came up with the notion of that protest flight to Washington to balance the negative headlines about the industry. What a lovely man, and what a very happy experience.

SLIDE: It's interesting that you are not political in your films, and then suddenly you are forcibly made political by the blacklist. And you end your film career with a political film, *Johnny Got His Gun* [1971].

HUNT: Oh please, I don't think I've ended my film career. It's just a long time between films! And I never thought of *Johnny Got His Gun* as political. It's a passionate cry against war, which must be a universal emotion. Dalton Trumbo was probably the best known and highest paid of the screenwriters grilled by the HUAC on their politics. And for not responding, he, with the others of "The Hollywood Ten," served time in prison, convicted of contempt of Congress. All of which made him a high-profile political figure.

Dalton's early novel *Johnny Got His Gun*, set around World War I, caused a sensation. Though fictional, he had woven many touches into it from his own life. He had long wanted it to be filmed, and finally determined to both write and direct it himself.

SLIDE: I remember seeing the film when I first came to this country. I don't remember it being very good, but I don't know why.

HUNT: The directing part was the pitfall. Dalton had never directed before, and this story was hideously challenging. What do you photograph when your central character is the ultimate "basket case"?—a young veteran without arms, legs, or face, only a wrapped torso and cranium. He can't hear, see, or speak. How to show his thoughts, memories, and nightmares? Undaunted, Dalton had to tackle it. The surprise is that it ever came out and proved as moving and well received as it was. But he'd had no sense of pace, didn't know the rudiments of film editing.

While wrestling with postproduction editing, Dalton called me and confessed that his film was far too long and he must somehow cut three hours out of it. They would include some scenes involving me, as Joe's mother, whole scenes making story-points, because he had just shot master scenes with no intercutting, reverse angles, etc. He was afraid some of my character now might not make sense, without those scenes. He was abject and humble about it. And yet, the film won something at the Cannes Film Festival, but it was for Dalton Trumbo, and because it was antiwar.

SLIDE: You understand a lot about directing. Did you ever want to be a director?

HUNT: I directed all the time as a child. If there wasn't a play going, I'd get a play started. I was always directing and/or acting. It never occurred to me to direct once I'd grown up. Isn't that funny? I've never been asked. People ask me if I've ever wanted to teach or coach acting. That hadn't occurred to me either. A good actor who happens to be articulate is a blend of two not necessarily compatible qualities. In fact, I remember the first Hollywood party I went to. It was given by the [Charles] Boyers, and it was filled with the top stars of Hollywood. I was so enthused and agog, trying not to show it, and waiting to hear all that witty dialogue. Well, I waited the whole evening, and I heard about the servant problem and where to shop. There wasn't a line to quote out of the entire evening. That's the night I came to respect the screenwriter. I realized all the wit was the writer's wit. Not the director's, not the players', but the writer's.

SLIDE: And that's why you married one [Robert Presnell, Jr.]?

HUNT: I didn't hold it against him. I must say, from then on, I really understood that the work of the actors, what makes them known to the public, is based on someone else's creative talent. And I don't think the public begins to understand that. If I resent anything, it's the title "auteur." The egos of directors require that they borrow identity to which they are not entitled. I want writers to get much tougher. When a television drama ends, I want to see "Written by." We have just experienced something, for better or worse, and if we hated it, I want to see who wrote this junk. And if we loved it, who wrote it? So we can respect and remember him.

I was nearly James Dean's mother in *Rebel without a Cause* [1954]. I was cast as the mother but had to pull out before shooting started because I was already committed to do *Anniversary Waltz* with Howard Duff at the Carthay Circle Theatre [in Los Angeles]. They were going to work their schedules so I could do both, and then each side toughened up and wouldn't give. I had to choose one or the other, and the mother was a terrible role. We were doing all our preproduction stills with the cast. Jim Backus as the father, me as the mother, and Jimmy Dean between us as our son. We were posing for pictures, and Dean was showing how disinterested he was, what a nonconformist he was. He'd never look at anybody, never talk to anybody, didn't acknowledge introductions. He was being as rude as possible. After a bit of this, I simply asked him whether he had enjoyed making a television show called *Something for an Empty Suitcase* as much as I had relished watching it. Suddenly, the eyes came into focus, and he looked at me as if I was a human being. I had remembered the writer's name. He said, "How can you remember the name of the writer?" "Because it impressed me so much, because it was a remarkable script." When we started talking about the program, I said, the way everyone moved, it was almost as if it were choreographed. It was not a musical, but there was a kind of rhythm, a grace, a kind of motion that everyone in it seemed to have. Well, we were off and running, and we had a relationship, because I could remember the title and the man who wrote the script. The writer should be named as soon as the work goes off the screen. That's who put it together; that's who conceived it out of air and put it on paper. Then all these other things happened to it. Now in the theatre, you don't take a comma away without the playwright's okay. I did get outraged as a writer's wife at the terrible lot they are accorded in this particular field.

MARC LAWRENCE

The pockmarked, olive-skinned gangster of so many Hollywood films of the 1930s and 1940s is also a gangster in the eyes of many liberals in Hollywood. Along with Larry Parks and Sterling Hayden, he is an actor who named names, and while his colleagues have long since received forgiveness, animosity toward Lawrence continues. It is unfair and unjust in that Marc Lawrence has suffered both financially and emotionally for what he did more than forty-five years ago, and as he indicates in our interview, the memory of that appearance before the House UnAmerican Activities Committee will haunt him for the rest of his life.

Born in New York—"I was a bright little Jew from the Bronx named Maxie Goldsmith"—Marc Lawrence became one of the thirty apprentices in Eva Le Gallienne's Repertory Theatre in 1931. The following year, he and a friend decided to try their luck in Hollywood, riding the rails for the journey west of Kansas City.

In 1932 Lawrence made his screen debut in Paramount's *If I Had a Million*, and gradually built up a reputation as a reliable character performer in villainous roles with films such as *Johnny Apollo* (1940), *Blossoms in the Dust* (1941), *This Gun for Hire* (1942), *The Ox-Bow Incident* (1943), *Key Largo* (1948), and *The Asphalt Jungle* (1950). Arguably, Lawrence's best Hollywood performance is as the gentle half-wit in *The Shepherd of the Hills* (1940).

Marc Lawrence married screenwriter Fanya Foss in Las Vegas on December 23, 1942; they had met at a screening of *Citizen Kane.*

On April 24, 1951, Marc Lawrence appeared in Washington, D.C., before the House UnAmerican Activities Committee. He admitted joining the Communist Party in 1932 because Lionel Stander had told him it was a good situation in which to "get to know dames." After attending twelve meetings, Lawrence quit the party in 1939. As he explained to the committee, "I just wanted to investigate and find out, not participate. I'm a curious kind of a schmo, the kind of guy who likes to listen to speeches and hear ideas defended. I didn't defend the ideas. I just listened and found it a very destructive thing and refused to participate." He named as fellow cell members J. Edward Bromberg, Morris Carnovsky, Lester Cole, Richard J. Collins, Jeff Corey, Gordon Kahn, John Howard Lawson, Karen Morley, Robert Rossen, and Lionel Stander. Lawrence also named, but did not identify as Communists, Howard Da Silva, Lloyd Gough, Sterling Hayden, Larry Parks, and Ann Revere. Two days later, Stander sued Lawrence for slander, asking half a million dollars in damages, but never pursued the suit.

On April 24, 1951, Lawrence and his wife left the United States for Europe. He became a popular leading man in Italian films, beginning with *Vacanze col Gangster* (also known as *Gun Moll*) in 1951. In 1958 Lawrence returned to the stage—in London—as Eddie Carbone in Arthur Miller's *A View from the Bridge*. In the 1960s Lawrence was back in the United States, producing and directing the 1963 feature film *Nightmare in the Sun*, and also directing episodes of the television series *Maverick*, *77 Sunset Strip*, *Roaring Twenties*, and *M Squad*. His later films as an actor include *The Kremlin Letter* (1970), *Marathon Man* (1976), *Foul Play* (1978), and *Ruby* (1992). As late as 1995, Lawrence was featured in the HBO movie *King of the Volcano*. In 1991 the actor self-published his autobiography, *Long Time No See: Confessions of a Hollywood Gangster*.

Marc Lawrence now lives in semiretirement in Palm Springs. His large house is as open and friendly as his sole companion, a small black poodle.

MARC LAWRENCE: I don't know what I'm going to tell you—probably a bunch of lies.

ANTHONY SLIDE: Did you find it a cathartic experience to write the autobiography?

LAWRENCE: At first I suppose it was. There was so much anger in me. It was really hard to face myself. I was sometimes talking to the mike, and I couldn't hear what I was saying. I was making a confession. That's how bad I felt. Why don't people talk to me anymore? Why don't I get jobs? What is the reason? Let's go back. Let's search that out. Let's look at me now. The first version of the book was so full of "Oh, my poor heart"—I had heart trouble as a kid, so I was dying all the time—and it was full of such tears, such self-pity. The first guy I showed it to was Ray Bradbury. Ray took me out to lunch, we drank a lot of wine, and he told me the truth. He said, "You've got to look for humor, step back a little, don't be so involved, look at yourself as some other person." Another friend helped me. He said, "Tell the truth; start with the Goddam testimony." I couldn't do that. I looked at the testimony, and I talked stupid. I was ashamed of what I said. I drank, but I wasn't drunk. I kept drinking through a whole bottle. I couldn't get drunk. I was stupefied, paralyzed.

SLIDE: But at the testimony you told the truth.

LAWRENCE: Richard Schickel is the guy who pointed out very clearly—as I do in the book when I quote him—that if there wasn't this fucking secret society, they would have nothing on 'em. Also, there were a lot of spies in this secret society that I never knew about.

SLIDE: Surely you must have known, because of the climate of the time, that the FBI was going to visit you?

LAWRENCE: No. I hadn't been to a meeting in years. I felt sorry for all those guys who were being called. A lot of people left [the Communist Party] in '41, but I sort of hung around. I kept listening to these guys. It made a lot of sense. They had a sense of nobility about themselves. There's nothing wrong about that. But they were agents like [Alger] Hiss—secret agents. I remember when I signed the stupid thing, the guy from New York said, "A signature is a signature for humanity." Oh Christ! I was being made a priest! This kind of approach, where you were signing your name for humanity. Bullshit! I never told anybody!

SLIDE: Why not?

LAWRENCE: Because you had to be careful—you were told to be careful.

SLIDE: But in your book, you write about being on the Columbia lot with Lionel Stander, and Harry Cohn coming along and asking why you were hanging around with a Red.

LAWRENCE: Lionel made no secret about his feelings to

anyone. He'd fart and say, "That's not me kid. It's all the shit I've been eating or taking." Lionel was very open about a lot of things.

SLIDE: Didn't Lionel Stander sue you after you named him as a Communist?

LAWRENCE: Sure he sued me.

SLIDE: Then he's a liar.

LAWRENCE: Sure. He wanted to protect himself. I like Lionel, despite all this. I liked a lot of guys. Sam Ornitz was a sweet man, a wonderful man, a serious dedicated man. John Howard Lawson was a serious, dedicated man. Dalton Trumbo, a lovely man. I liked him. This is an interview? You want to get quotes?

SLIDE: I want to go back now in time.

LAWRENCE: Back, back, back.

SLIDE: You worked with Paul Muni in the Jewish theatre in New York?

LAWRENCE: No, my uncle did. I had an uncle who was a star with Paul Muni. They were buddies. My uncle saw me act in high school and said, "When you get through college, I'll take care of your career." But he died in my sophomore year. He was thirty-nine. My name then was Goldsmith, M. Lawrence Goldsmith. I was given the name Lawrence when I went to high school by a guy who taught me math. When I did the first play on Broadway, *Thomas Paine*, a producer put the name of Marc Lawrence in the program. I got good reviews. I remember one critic saying, "Just too much Paine." Oh yes, Paul Muni . . . Muni was appearing in a play, *This Man Saul* [1929], written by Sidney Buchman, who eventually became one of Harry Cohn's writers. I sent my name, Goldsmith, backstage, and Muni came out. "Goldsmith, where's Goldsmith?" he said. He looked at me and hugged me. He takes me in his dressing room and tells me the story. I'm not even listening to him because I'm replacing Muni in the role of my uncle. He's going to take care of me. I'm just imagining all the things he's going to do for me. I ask him, "What school do you follow, Mr. Muni?" "The Duse school." I say, "Duse who?" That was more or less the end. I felt forsaken.

SLIDE: Eva Le Gallienne. From today's viewpoint, one sees Eva Le Gallienne and her company as a group of rather sensitive performers. Then you appear to change character totally when you come to Hollywood.

LAWRENCE: I was made part of the company. And one summer, my friend Artie Liebowitz, who was a neighbor, said, "Your brother's out in California. Let's go to California." I said, "Wait 'til I've had breakfast." I thought he was kidding. We took the subway downtown. He picked up a newspaper and read that a guy wanted a car driven to Kansas City. We called the guy, drove the car to Kansas City, and that was the end of the journey. I planned to come back for the winter because Richard Waring and I were the two chosen for the company. We'd get paid twenty-five dollars. Burgess Meredith was a second-year apprentice. One of the students was John Garfield, but he didn't make it. I was one of the two of thirty who made it. So while I was waiting the summer out, I came here and did something. Then I heard Le Gallienne had an accident, and she disbanded the company for a year.

SLIDE: That's when you decided to stay here?

LAWRENCE: I gave a recital. I went to some theatre on Hollywood Boulevard and said, "I want to give a recital." I read from *The Last Mile*. I did some impersonations of actors very badly. I had a lot of courage. Okay, an agent saw me and said, "You're either crazy or you have a lot of talent." He brought me out to see William Wyler, who was casting a picture called *Laughing Boy*. He liked me. I was a skinny kid with black eyes, black hair, a very thin face. He gave me a script, I picked out a scene in pantomime, and he was much impressed. He welcomed me, and I felt welcome. He left town, and two weeks later, when he came back, he shelved the picture. So I had lunch with him, and during lunch I fainted because I was taking so much California sun. I think he left me a ten-dollar bill. That was the end of my relationship.

SLIDE: Did you regret that you became typecast in Hollywood?

LAWRENCE: In a way I disliked it. Because I was more a character actor. I never wanted to play Hamlet. Everybody wanted to be a gangster. Jimmy Cagney. Eddy Robinson. Eddy was a fantastic actor. My God, he ate the screen up.

SLIDE: Did you try to emulate them?

LAWRENCE: Of course you try to emulate them in some way.

Like the kids today hear music and they want to play the music, whether it's lousy or loud. So I'm watching these marvelous actors play these tough guys. I used to smoke a lot in order to make my voice deeper. I remember the first important job I got was with Gene Raymond in *If I Had a Million*. Jimmy Cruze was the director. I thought Gene Raymond was lousy, a lousy actor. What was he doing playing the lead? So I went the next day—this is the nerve I had then—and I waited to see Mr. Cruze. The assistant director came and asked, "What are you doing here?" So I told him I wanted to replace Gene Raymond. He was very patient with me and explained why I couldn't do it.

SLIDE: Was Gene Raymond really a bad actor?

LAWRENCE: No. I just could have been better. Ego! There was something in my character that was ambitious, blindly ambitious.

SLIDE: Later, when you wanted to play the Boris Karloff role in *Penitentiary* [1938], a remake of *The Criminal Code*, was that also ego?

LAWRENCE: Yes. I imitated Karloff very badly. Harry Cohn loved me for some reason or another. I'll tell you what it was. Johnny Roselli. Do you know who he was? He was hired by the FBI to knock off Castro. Harry Cohn was a real gangster, a real tough guy, and he was sitting in his projection room with a tougher guy, Johnny Roselli. I came on the screen, and Roselli bends over to Harry and says, "That kid up there, the skinny one, you could take him for one of the mob." Harry was so impressed. I felt as if I could get anything from the studio. I went in and said, I want a part. "You got it! Now get out! I'm busy!" I went to be interviewed by a director at the annex of Columbia Studios. I was sitting in the projection room in whatever row it was, and a voice behind me says, "I couldn't hear you last time." It was Harry Cohn. So I went over, hit him in the belly, and said, "You're getting fat, Harry." He said, "When you get through here, you drive me back to the studio," which was about four blocks. I said, "The amount you're paying me, you want me to be your chauffeur!" That was the arrogance I had. I believed my own stupid make-believe. Later on, later on, after I left Columbia, I played *Golden Boy* [on the stage in Los Angeles in 1939]. I played Eddy Fuselli, the gangster. Stella Adler directed it, and Frances Lederer played Golden Boy. Anyway,

Ed Sullivan put together a whole column about the tough guys, and he said the only man who could come on the screen without makeup was Marc Lawrence. This kind of shit.

SLIDE: Which other gangsters did you meet?

LAWRENCE: Bugsy Siegel. In the '30s, we belonged to a club on Roxbury Drive, and I remember one night I was with Virginia Hill. We went to Rudolph Valentino's home, Falcon's Lair, that Bugsy was renting. And they had an American-Chinese girl for me, a beautiful dame. I'm in Rudolph Valentino's bedroom that's about as big as a football field. And in the midst of going down on me, she looks up and says, "I can't believe it's you, Mr. Lawrence."

SLIDE: The gangsters you knew, did they teach you anything about how to play a part?

LAWRENCE: No. I think there was something in my character that was ambitious, blindly ambitious.

SLIDE: I was reading an article in which you said you had a psychological and dramatic approach to acting.

LAWRENCE: What does that mean?

SLIDE: I was going to ask you what it meant.

LAWRENCE: If I said that, I don't know what I was talking about. It's a bullshit answer. I learned a lot of things technically from a man named Michael Chekhov. He taught me more about acting than anyone else. And it's true, the more I think about it, even when Marty Landau talks about the acting that he learned from that horrible man, Lee Strasberg. When I met Mr. Chekhov, he said, all acting is legato and staccato. That put it into a nutshell. I remember [Laurence] Olivier and [Dustin] Hoffman were doing a scene in *Marathon Man*, and [director John] Schlessinger would say, "Larry, cut the next line, then go back." And, "Larry, the next two lines are not necessary." Finally, Olivier got so mad and said, "I cannot cut what I have already learned. If you have to cut it, cut it in the cutting room." He was right! So, coming back to Chekhov, the rhythm of speech is important. With rhythm, I can talk fast, I can move fast. Or talk slowly. Visually and vocally, I am changing rhythms. All good acting is legato or staccato. Marlon Brando, the great discovery of Lee Strasberg, made a damn stink about this. I don't put him down because a lot of people respected him. Stella Adler didn't, and Stella was a good friend of mine.

SLIDE: Today, so many actors say they cannot play a part unless they research the character. Is this true for you?

LAWRENCE: Not really. If you get an image, the image is clearer than you. You only have to imitate the image. If only you can be partially as good as the image. Research—the intellectuals like that. That's fine. Olivier, who I think is the most brilliant actor, didn't do that. For some reason, I hear more to it because of my heart. I had a heart murmur as a kid, and I still have an irregular heartbeat. The more I do it technically, the less wear and tear. It's easy for me to cry. In *Shepherd of the Hills*, when I was shot as this mute by Beulah Bondi, Beulah said to me, when it came to the close-up, "Teach me how to cry; make me cry." Instinctively, I just took her, held her close, and walked away.

SLIDE: You've worked with some pretty tough directors, people like William Wellman, John Huston, Henry Hathaway.

LAWRENCE: I compared Wellman to Toscanini. He had a goosing stick. And he didn't like interference. He'd chase the assistant director off the set because he didn't want any of Darryl Zanuck's stooges around. Wellman was an extraordinary person. He was a man who loved movies, who loved making movies, just as Huston loved making movies. Joe von Sternberg was an interesting man, a tyrant but interesting. He loved what I did. He saw me in *Golden Boy* and liked the character. A monster, a terrible guy, but he made me feel like a big star. He took me to his house in Reseda. He said, "Only great people can sit in this chair." He said, "Only three people have faces like yours: Garbo, Marlene Dietrich, and you." A load of nonsense.

SLIDE: Do you prefer a tough director? Do you like a director who tells you what to do?

LAWRENCE: I'd rather he kissed my ass. Just love me, make love to me, and leave me alone. I don't like anybody to tell me what to do.

SLIDE: What about Henry Hathaway?

LAWRENCE: Hathaway was an asshole. He didn't want me in *Shepherd of the Hills*. He said, "How can a Jew play a hillbilly?" This kind of shit. Then he said, "I'm one-fourth Jewish; it's nothing against Jews." I did a couple of other things for Henry. He was tough on the set. Henry gave me a script for

Ten Gentlemen from West Point [1942]. He said, "Read this as if you were directing it, Marc, and make notes." So I worked on it. He said, "That's exactly what I'm thinking, exactly my idea." I said, "Henry, I'm not in competition with you." Then he confessed to me after the second or third script we worked on. "You know my best picture? My best picture was *Lives of a Bengal Lancer* [1934]. You know why? Because I had my good luck disease. I had shingles. Every time I do a picture, I get mad at people because I want to re-create the same feeling I had when I did *Lives of a Bengal Lancer.*" Poor Henry is in search of a lost itch. I liked Henry. He had a boyish quality about him. But he never accepted my reversals. He never accepted me as a person after the investigation. The only man who ever did was an actor called Louis Calhern. Bless him! Louis invited me to his house, and we had dinner. He was a prince.

SLIDE: How do you think some people avoided being called before the committee?

LAWRENCE: Some people were paid off. Some had protectors. Some of the guys had to testify behind closed door. I'm not going to name anybody. It killed a lot of people, because the fucking Commies said, "Keep your fucking mouths shut."

SLIDE: Who are you actually blaming for the work of the House UnAmerican Activities Committee?

LAWRENCE: I blame the Commies.

SLIDE: How can you blame the Communists? Nobody forced you to become a member.

LAWRENCE: That in essence is true, but it's not true. If you join the church and you believe in the church, how the fuck can you tell me not to believe in it. I believed in the future they talked about. And I felt guilty because I was under contract making money. All this bullshit. It was a ploy. They wanted to get into the government, and they wanted to get all the propaganda they could get from Hollywood.

SLIDE: In reality, how could anyone in Hollywood change the system?

LAWRENCE: They couldn't. The point is that in making it a secret society, they made it treacherous. Where there's smoke, there's fire; and where there's silence, there's guilt. If it was an open society, they wouldn't have to ask you who was a member of the Communist Party. They could look it up.

SLIDE: You appeared before the committee and said you joined the party in order to meet girls. Stupid?

LAWRENCE: No. That was my way of trying to escape. I didn't know if I was going to talk or not up to the very minute. But the pressure was so strong, absolutely overpowering. To defy anybody, you have to be a Lionel Stander, you have to be a Lillian Hellman. And Lillian Hellman came two years after me. You have to be a Morris Carnovsky, who believed. God bless them for believing. I didn't believe. My wife was bewildered by the whole thing.

SLIDE: Was your wife a member of the party?

LAWRENCE: No. She refused to join. Poor Fanya.

SLIDE: Was it harder for her than for you?

LAWRENCE: In certain ways I guess it was. I'm crying because I miss her. [At this point, Marc Lawrence broke down, and we took a break from recording.] You want to cut my heart.

SLIDE: The people that you named, had they been named before?

LAWRENCE: Most of them were.

SLIDE: When you appeared before the committee, did you know you were going to have to name names?

LAWRENCE: I kept drinking, not wanting to face what I had to face. I was going to be a tough guy, and I was going to go to Europe the next day. That was my plan. I told Julie [John] Garfield the night before—I met him in a restaurant—and he said, "Fuck them all." I fell on my face. I kept drinking to give me courage, but it never gave me courage. It deadened all my senses. I was empty. I wish I could have believed. I would have said, "Fuck you. I played the gangsters, and you're the gangsters now. Get off my back. If you want to burn me, put a fire under me and burn me." I should have said that and walked out.

SLIDE: You are hard on yourself.

LAWRENCE: Of course I am.

SLIDE: At least you had the courage to go before the committee. Look at Berthold Brecht, who fled the country rather than appear.

LAWRENCE: None of these guys had the courage to say, "I am a Communist. I believe in communism. It's as true as Americanism. I believe in America and I believe in communism too, like you believe in being a Democrat." Why didn't they say that? They had been told to keep quiet. I can see it plainly now.

SLIDE: In 1953 you felt you had been cleared?

LAWRENCE: I got a call from some guy at the FBI. He says, "Have you got anything else to say, Mr. Lawrence?" I said, "Can you get me a job? Nobody's offering me one." He said, "I'm sorry to hear that." That was his answer. So I hung up. That was my answer. When you come to Italy, you have to check in with the police. When you leave America, you have to check in with the FBI.

SLIDE: Did you enjoy the years in Italy?

LAWRENCE: Italy was a savior to me. As Hemingway said, it's like having died and gone to heaven. I couldn't believe the adulation they gave me. The director kissing my hand. People running after me. I was mistaken for Gary Cooper! You see, the moment an American actor came to town in Italy, there would be big headlines in the paper. I was much happier in Europe than I was in America. I never felt at home in America. Still don't. I'm living in a place with iron bars on it.

SLIDE: Why did you return?

LAWRENCE: I think mysteriously you hope something will disappear, but it doesn't disappear. All these scars I had on my face. My long nose. When I came back to America, I had my nose made shorter and the scars removed. This was my bread and butter! And I got less and less work.

SLIDE: When you came back over here, you changed careers and started to direct.

LAWRENCE: I told Harry Cohn I wanted to be a director. He said, "Get out of here. Stay where you belong." That was accidental. In desperation, I called Max Shane, who was producing *M Squad*, and I said, "I need a job." He wrote something for me, and I went to do it on the set with Lee Marvin. Lee liked the way I did the scene, and at the end of the day he said, "Let's have a drink." From there, I did two *M Squads*. Then I went to Warners and I did a *Roaring Twenties*, I did eighteen *Lawmen*, I did *77 Sunset Strip*, I did a couple of comedies. Then I went to Metro to do *Rawhide* with Clint Eastwood. I was fired after three days. Why? Because I changed the scene to one that was not in the script.

SLIDE: Then you made *Nightmare in the Sun*?

LAWRENCE: Yeah. I met a girl who put up the money, the

quarter of a million dollars, and I got all these stars—Sammy Davis Jr., Keenan Wynn, Robert Duvall—to do bits for me. The gal who gave me the money was a DuPont, and she wanted her name on the screen. I said, "I can't. If all these guys knew the money came from a millionaire, they'd cut my throat. If I sell the picture and your name is on the screen, I won't get a penny for it." Then I cut in John Derek as my partner because he gave me Ursula Andress, who was a hot girl then. He said, "Let's do a nude scene." I thought, Jesus, if she does a nude scene at the beginning when Aldo Ray rapes her, I'll sell the picture. The day before we started to shoot, he changed his mind. When I got a fifty thousand dollar note to get out of the picture, they put in a nude scene. I don't want to go into that shit.

SLIDE: As you get older, is it more difficult to get parts?

LAWRENCE: I don't want to act anymore. I have enough money. I'm comfortable. I acted last year in *Gotti* [a made-for-television movie], and they cut the heart out of my scene. When I saw this, I thought, what am I doing here? I said, "Take my name off the screen. I don't want to be associated with this." Enough of this shit.

SLIDE: Looking back, would you have done it the same way?

LAWRENCE: No. I wish I could have told a lot of the people to go fuck themselves. I should have told the committee to go fuck themselves. I would have walked out a hero. I would have been comfortable with myself for the rest of my life. I would have been happy with myself as a human being. I torture myself when people look at me as if I were a fink.

SLIDE: Does it still hurt you?

LAWRENCE: Sure it still hurts me. I'm eighty-seven years old, and I don't like that feeling. They never forget. It's like a tattoo. You can't take it off. What else can I tell you? I didn't want to do it, but I didn't have the strength. I was just overwhelmed. I wish I could tell you some other bullshit.

DORIS NOLAN

It is unfortunate that Doris Nolan is best remembered for her performance as Katharine Hepburn's sister—the woman to whom Cary Grant is engaged—in *Holiday* (1938). Here, she is patrician, regal and icy cold, characteristics that are very much the opposite to the "real" Doris Nolan, who is easygoing, fun loving, vibrant, and energetic. As our interview indicates, she is a woman very willing to speak her mind on a variety of subjects. She is enthusiastic in her likes and strong willed and obstinate in her dislikes. Doris Nolan is a woman one would definitely want to have on one's side in a fight. While she jokes of her nervousness on stage, often viewing theatre and films as a necessary chore, Doris Nolan is a consummate actress. She may laugh at her mistakes or her occasional gauche behavior in her chosen profession; but she has done nothing of which to be ashamed either in public or in private, and she has accomplished much of which to be proud.

Born in New Rochelle, New York, on July 14, 1916, Ms. Nolan began to study for a professional career on stage immediately after graduation from high school. Her first foray into the motion picture industry in 1933–1934, when she was under contract to Fox at one hundred fifty dollars a week, was an unmitigated disaster. But she followed that with her first Broadway production, *Night of January 16th*, which ran for a year and was followed by *Arrest That Woman* (1936), *Tell Me Pretty Maiden* (1937), and *Lorelei* (1938).

In 1936 Doris Nolan returned to Hollywood, under contract to Universal, and made her screen debut in *The Man I Marry* (1937). The studio embarked on a major publicity campaign to promote the actress as a new, rising star, but films such as *As Good As Married* (1937), *Top of the Town* (1937), and *One Hour to Live* (1939) did nothing to enhance her reputation. Universal simply failed to give her the roles or the productions that she deserved and that would have helped her shine as a light comedienne in the manner of Carole Lombard or Jean Arthur. Ms. Nolan's role in *Holiday* was the most important in the actress's feature films, but it was as the second lead, in support of Katharine Hepburn. In later films, *Irene* (1940) and *Moon over Burma* (1940), Ms. Nolan would be similarly cast, supporting such luminaries as Anna Neagle and Dorothy Lamour. Her American film career ended in 1943 with *Follies Girl*.

However, while her screen career was winding down, Doris Nolan remained in demand in the theatre. In 1940 she embarked on the first of a series of tours, playing the actress Loraine Sheldon in *The Man Who Came to Dinner* by George S. Kaufman and Moss Hart. Initially, she appeared opposite Alexander Woollcott, on whom the central character was based, and later worked with the play's authors, Laird Cregar and Clifton Webb. Ms. Nolan also enjoyed a major success on Broadway, starring from 1942 to 1943 in *Doughgirls*, written by Joe Fields and Moss Hart, and directed by George S. Kaufman.

On December 30, 1944, Doris Nolan married Alexander Knox [1907–1995], a serious and dedicated actor whose Hollywood films include *None Shall Escape* (1944), *Wilson* (1944), *Sister Kenny* (1946), and *The Judge Steps Out* (1948). Coincidentally, the date in the title of Doris Nolan's first Broadway appearance, *Night of January 16th*, was also the date of Alexander Knox's birth. In 1949 Doris Nolan and Alexander Knox starred together on Broadway in *The Closing Door*, written by Knox. The actor was a supporter of liberal causes, very active with the Committee for the First Amendment. He is "named" by Myron C. Fagan in *Documentation of the Red Stars in Hollywood* (Hollywood: Cinema Educational Guild, 1950) because of his involvement with the Actors' Lab, the American Russian Institute, the Committee for the First Amendment, and the Progressive Citizens of America. As a Canadian, Knox had little choice but to leave the United States as the political situation deteriorated. The initial move was in 1950, when Knox was invited to star in London in *Return to Tyassi*, written by Benn Levy and costarring Levy's wife, Constance Cummings. With his wife and their son Andrew, he moved permanently to England in the early 1950s. Doris Nolan became involved in other pursuits, but she continued to act, appearing on stage and television, and in small parts in a handful of British films, including Joseph Losey's *The Servant* (1973) and *The Romantic Englishwoman* (1975).

After commuting between a London apartment and a tower home at Bamburgh Castle in Northumberland, Alexander Knox and Doris Nolan took up permanent residence in 1972 in the Scottish border town of Berwick-upon-Tweed. It is there that Doris Nolan and I spoke together.

ANTHONY SLIDE: Was your family middle class?

DORIS NOLAN: Yes, they were middle class. We had a small house in New Rochelle, with a garden, a dog, and a cat. I had a younger sister and an older brother.

SLIDE: How and why did you decide to become an actress?

NOLAN: It wasn't my decision really. I didn't have any choice. In high school, we had an English drama teacher who was very enthusiastic about the theatre, and he began to get me to read plays. I'd never been to see a play in New York, but I always seemed to get the leads in school plays, and the local papers said, "This girl has a nice voice, a pleasing personality. She should be an actress. We think she might have a future." Well, at that time, my father's business had gone bankrupt, and we were a little bit on our uppers. I wanted to go to college, but I don't think they could have afforded it. The drama teacher said, "Why don't you have a go at a drama school in New York?" I didn't have enough money to go to the American Academy of Dramatic Arts, but we saw an advertisement in the paper for this small drama school down at the Greenwich Village Playhouse, where Eugene O'Neill had done his productions. At the time, the theatre was derelict, but this chap, an English actor named Reginald Goode—he was a bit of a ham actor—rented the top of the theatre. He had a very small company, at the most twelve pupils at a time. I went for an interview and said I didn't have very much money. They didn't have grants, so he said, "Can you do shorthand and typing?" I said, "Yes," because I had taken a business course at high school. He said, "Okay, if you pay just a small sum and do some secretarial work for me and my wife, you can come." He auditioned me, and obviously I had some talent. Anyway, he turned out to be a very good teacher. He had a lot of imagination, and he used the improvisation method, but not like that awful man who I hate, Lee Strasberg. He'd get three sets of us standing up, and he'd have us do a scene, say, from *The Taming of the Shrew*, all at once, in loud voices. The rest of the pupils had to sit in the class and laugh, react to us. So we lost our self-consciousness. It was very relaxing. What happened was that the audience developed these hilarious big laughs—that's where I got this awful hoot that I do. It really is terrible, but it's quite funny. I used it later in *The Man Who Came to Dinner* in a scene with Alexander Woollcott, and it used to bring down the house. The audience used to laugh until they practically peed in their pants.

What Reginald Goode did with us was very good. We used to go around and do charity performances at all sorts of places, where elderly or poor people lived, anywhere we could get an audience. We would play for free and put on, say, a program of three one-act plays in an evening. Then, after they were all over, he'd say, "Now, ladies and gentlemen, I'm going to ask you to propose a problem for two or three of these actors, and they will improvise a play for you." We'd have to improvise the whole thing for about half an hour. It was great fun and good exercise for the brain. Then he rented a summer theatre in Clinton Hollow, New York. He had a little bungalow and a little theatre, and, as a star pupil, I stayed with him and his wife and another actress in the bungalow. I played all the leads in the plays that summer.

A casting man came up from Fox and offered me a screen test. We were at Clinton Hollow all summer, so I went down in the autumn and did a screen test in New York. I had a terrible accident. I fell upstairs and knocked all my teeth and loosened them. I had one black tooth in front, my hair was lank and dingy, and I must have looked like a witch. Anyway, I got the contract with Fox for one hundred fifty dollars a week. I would have been sixteen and a half years old.

There was a big crisis with the family because they didn't want me to go out there alone. I was too young. So my family nicely suggested that my mother come out for six months and live with me for the duration of the contract, and my sister would have to run the house. Fox had a little acting school, and they put me in a class with the trainees. There must have been six or eight of us in this class. Rita Hayworth was in the class.

She was the homeliest girl in the class. She was fat. She had hair all over and wore it down over her forehead. Her eyebrows were thick. She was so shy, she could hardly speak. You would have thought she was the most unlikely girl to succeed in the world. Lillian Barkley was the teacher. Shirley Temple was the big star at Fox, and Lillian was her coach. Lillian gave me a few tests, but I didn't like acting much in front of the camera. I got a few extra jobs, just bit parts. Lillian took me under her wing and introduced me to Shirley Temple's mother. We became very friendly with them.

SLIDE: Were they nice people?

NOLAN: Very nice. Shirley was very bright. Oh gosh, she was quick in the head. They used to think she was a dwarf, she was so smart.

SLIDE: She wasn't arrogant because of her stardom?

NOLAN: No. And her mother was a very sensible woman. They liked me, so Shirley suggested I play with her in this film [*Our Little Girl*, 1935]. Shirley was supposed to have run away, and for some reason, I was a nurse who found her and had to bring her home. We got on the set that morning. They had whisked me through makeup too fast, and when I went on the set, my hair was sort of wet, still hanging down. I was very up-set about that. I had to take Shirley by the hand, open the door, and go into the living room where her parents were standing, hit my mark, and say some lines. Well, I'd open the door and walk in. I wouldn't hit my mark, so they had to cut. Try again! I open the door, walk in, hit my mark, and forget my line. I was in an absolute sweat. It's a terrible thing, facing the camera for the first time in a big production. And Shirley was getting impatient. We went out, and she said, "Listen, take me by the hand, I'll take you in, I'll get you on your mark, and I'll kick you when you have to say your line." Off we go again, and, of course, I blew it. I must have done five takes, and they finally said, "Cut. We'll go to another scene." I was fired immediately. That was the end of my screen career! When the contract was up in six months, they dropped me.

I was going right back to New York with nothing to do, when my agent called and said, "There's a play going on." It was called *Arrest That Woman*. It was a melodrama. There were drugs involved, and this, that, and the other. I can't remember much about it except that I had a very dramatic part. I guess it played for a week or two. And a very famous producer from New York called A. H. Woods, Al Woods, had turned up and seen it. He offered me a contract to take this play to New York and play it on Broadway. That was big excitement! When we got to New York, he decided not to do *Arrest That Woman*. It was too old-fashioned. He had this script by a famous woman called Ayn Rand, who was a very right-wing writer. Politically, that was bad, but I didn't know anything about politics at the time. It was a courtroom drama called *Night of January 16th*. It was a very imaginative idea. We were the witnesses, and they drew the jury from the audience. They had a big drum in the lobby, and if you wanted to be on the jury, you put your name in this thing. Of course, they cheated all the time. If Jack Dempsey was there, or some screen star, they'd always be sure to get him on the jury. The curtain would go up on the empty stage, and they'd pick out the jury. They'd file up and get into the witness box, and then the actors would come on and the play would start. Great fun! At the end, the jury would go out with the foreman, who was part of the cast, and they'd decide. There were two endings to the play—guilty or not guilty. So we had different juries and different endings every night. We began rehearsals, and here I was, seventeen years old, playing the part of the mistress of a famous Swedish match king, a multimillionaire. I was supposed to be a femme fatale, probably mid-thirties, very chic. It was very odd casting.

SLIDE: Did you actually look the part?

NOLAN: Yes. On stage I always looked older. I never played an ingenue part in my life because I always had a rather big, heavy voice, and it wasn't suitable for ingenues. Walter Pidgeon was cast in one of the leading roles. Sarah Padden, a character actress, was in it. Edmund Breese was the prosecuting attorney. It was a good cast. We were going out of town, to Philadelphia and some other place, for tryouts. We started rehearsals, and I wasn't rehearsing very well. I didn't seem to be hitting the part at all. I was very nervous, what with my first Broadway production and being so young. I had a long part, and I had a very big, dramatic, hysterical scene. Al Woods must have had over fifty percent in the show, but the Shubert Brothers had an interest and they had the theatre. I was making a mess of things, and somebody said, "This girl is hopeless." The Shuberts began to come to rehearsals, and they would bring other leading actresses in, naturally without letting me know, to watch me rehearse. Tallulah Bankhead came once. They wanted to fire me. Well, I must admit Al Woods stuck by me. I don't know why, but he'd seen me play this dramatic part in Hollywood. During rehearsals, he suggested that Sarah Padden take me through the part and coach me. She took me home for about three or four evenings, gave me a drink of whiskey, and took me through the part. She said, "Don't just stand there and mumble; start to play it." I went back and did that, and things were going along better, but the Shuberts still wanted to get rid of me up to the last minute. Well, to cut a long story short, opening night came, and I was sitting in the dressing room with the girl who played the widow. I was in such a state of nerves. I said, "I'm going to leave the theatre, I can't go on." I was making up, and I had this razor in my hand, cutting up an eyebrow pencil. What did I do? I cut my thumb. A big, huge cut, with blood all over the place. I had this huge bandage on my right thumb. They had to put glue on it or something to stop the bleeding. I was shaking like a leaf. But I forgot all my troubles because I was worrying about my thumb. In the dramatic scene, I was crying like mad because my thumb hurt so. The Shuberts came back afterwards and apologized to me. They said they were glad I was in it. The play was a hit.

SLIDE: You were under contract to Al Woods?

NOLAN: Yes, he was my manager.

SLIDE: So he decided what would be the next step in your career?

NOLAN: He sure did—and it was a big mistake. I had offers from M-G-M, Warners, and Universal. I think M-G-M and Warners offered seven hundred fifty or a thousand dollars a week, and Universal offered fifteen hundred a week. So he sold me to Universal. My parents and I knew nothing about the movies, so we said okay. I didn't know what the good film companies were, and we picked the worst one. If I'd gone to M-G-M, it really would have been a different story because they would have groomed me in small parts first and gradually moved me along. Al Woods had fifty percent of my contract, even when he sold me. I think he had control of Claudette

Colbert and Tyrone Power at one time, but they were lucky because the studios bought out their contracts with him. Universal didn't buy out my contract. Those contracts were legal at that time. I was the first one who had to break that type of contract, and it took years of litigation.

SLIDE: From *Night of January 16th* you went directly back to Hollywood?

NOLAN: That's right. The play went on tour, but Al was anxious to make money out of me so he dumped me on Universal. My sister went out with me this time. She'd do secretarial work. She used to sign my autographs for me— don't tell anybody! The first thing they told me was that I had to lose twenty pounds. So I went on this awful diet, exercised, and rode horseback, and I think I went down from a hundred and thirty to one hundred and ten pounds. I got very thin in the face and very tired. They did screen tests and bleached my hair. I'm a light brunette—mousey color. They tried wigs and everything because my hair was always pretty flimsy. They always bleached people's hair at that time because it was better to be a blonde in black-and-white films. There was a director at the studio at that time, Gregory La Cava, who was doing a film with Carole Lombard and Adolphe Menjou—*My Man Godfrey* [1936]. Lombard was supposed to have a sister. They wanted a brunette, and they'd just blonded my hair. They did a screen test, and Greg La Cava looked at it. I did photograph well. I was very photogenic. I looked much better on the screen than I did off. But he said, "No, she looks too much like Lombard, and Lombard won't like it." So they got another girl, Evelyn Venable. Anyway, I got to meet Gregory La Cava, with whom I fell madly in love. He was a man much older than I was. I guess he was in his early forties, and I was only eighteen at that time.

SLIDE: You moved in with La Cava?

NOLAN: No, never. You didn't in those days. I just went around with him all the time.

SLIDE: Did he become your mentor?

NOLAN: No, he wasn't any good for my career at all. He never put me in a film. He just diverted my mind from what I was doing.

SLIDE: He didn't give you advice?

NOLAN: I never asked him. I was never like Paulette Goddard or somebody who was very smart and clever. I was never shrewd. I just didn't want to ask him to do anything. I think if he had asked me to do a film with him, I wouldn't have done it. Crazy! Everybody thought I was going around with him because he was a big director, but I was just madly in love with him.

SLIDE: Tell me a little bit about La Cava.

NOLAN: When I met him, I was eighteen years old and very naive. He looked like a better-looking version of Frank Capra. He was of Italian descent. He was a loner. He didn't like to be tied up with a studio for too long. He'd been married and had two sons. He never talked about them. He kept supporting them all the time. I never had any curiosity about these things, and I never asked. His business woman always paid the wife. I found him very glamorous because he wore a beret, cashmere sweaters, beautiful slacks, and Gucci shoes. He was neat and trim. In those days, you didn't live together, but for the summer he'd rent a beach house down in Malibu and I'd sometimes go down for the weekends. We'd have chaperones. He was a drinker. At that time I didn't drink at all, but he did teach me to drink Scotch. He was fun, and he was funnier when he'd had a few drinks. He had a wonderful sense of humor. I can't remember discussing politics with him, but we used to go around with Adolphe Menjou and his wife, and agent Myron Selznick and his actress wife Josephine Hutchinson.

SLIDE: What happened next at Universal?

NOLAN: Finally, they put me in a film called *The Man I Married*. A "B" picture. They only put me in one "A" picture. *The Man I Married* was directed by Ralph Murphy, who was not a very well known director. He was a nice chap. He was competent, I suppose. Michael Whalen was the leading man. He wasn't up to much. I remember Nigel Bruce. We were doing a wedding scene, and he had to say a line, "Are you going to Connecticut for your honeymoon?" And for some reason he couldn't say "Connecticut." We had to do about ten takes.

SLIDE: This is your first film, and it's a rowdy comedy. Did you want to be a comedienne?

NOLAN: Well, I played comedy in summer stock. I was at the

point where I just did what I was told. I was only eighteen years old, and I knew nothing.

SLIDE: Your next film was *Top of the Town* [1937].

NOLAN: They had a scenic designer, who was very new at the time and very hot. He did silly things. He obviously wasn't used to film. He must have come from the stage. He had real-life oranges hanging from trees, which would melt during shooting. I read the script, and I said, "I can't do it. This is ghastly. Here I am, a dramatic actress, and you're having me waltz through as a rich society lady, doing nothing. I'm surrounded by singers and dancers. Nothing to do!" Universal said they had groomed me for stardom, that this was a big production, and I had to do it.

SLIDE: You didn't sing in the film?

NOLAN: I couldn't sing. I couldn't dance. I just wore these costumes, all these fancy clothes. I was surrounded by comedians, the equivalent of goons. I was beautifully photographed, but I had absolutely nothing to do except walk through it. The picture was a crashing failure. It was a big flop. What saved the studio at the time was Deanna Durbin. They gave her good scripts and good directors. I destroyed the studio and she saved it. It didn't do any good for my ego. After that, I did *As Good As Married* [1937], directed by Eddie Buzzell, a "B" director, too. They wouldn't give me any of the good directors, any of the good scripts.

SLIDE: You had a couple of good leading men—Walter Pidgeon and John Boles.

NOLAN: John Boles wasn't a very good actor. He was a nice man, had a good singing voice, but he wasn't a very good actor.

SLIDE: At some point during this time, you must have gone back to New York and stage.

NOLAN: That's right. When Woods signed the contract with Universal, he had the right every six months to bring me back to do a stage play. I liked that because I loved to go back on the stage. Unfortunately, he picked . . . I seem to have had a long career of flops. It wasn't my fault, because other people had control over me, and I had to do what I was told. Otherwise I didn't work. Al Woods revived a thriller, *Arrest That Woman*. It was a crashing failure. Terrible! It was one of those dreadful opening nights that you think can't happen. It was pouring rain, and everyone who came in was soaking wet. It was a wild, old-fashioned melodrama, where I had to shoot somebody. And, of course, the gun didn't go off. It went off ten minutes later. The curtain came down before the scene was finished, so nobody knew what happened—the poor actors, having to appear in this trash. This was one of Hugh Marlowe's first plays—nice chap. The rest of the cast was just terrible. I mean, the audience was laughing during the play. Al Woods had booked the theatre, I guess, for about four weeks. I was in a terrible state. I went back home to New Rochelle, and I said to my parents, "I cannot play this for four weeks. We've got to do something about it." They didn't know anything about the theatre, but they asked Al Woods to come up one weekend. He was a bad dresser, he dressed very sloppily, and underneath his trousers, he had his pajamas hanging down, and he had his slippers on. I can't remember very much about the interview, but we closed in two weeks. Hugh Marlowe never forgave me for it because he lost two weeks' salary. I think I went back and did a thriller, *One Hour to Live* [1939], another "B" picture.

SLIDE: Then back to the stage for *Tell Me Pretty Maiden.*

NOLAN: *Tell Me Pretty Maiden* was so close to being a hit, it was heartbreaking. It was about an actress who came from a poor background, like the Bronx, and she gives her first interview. It opens with her all done up like a leading actress, surrounded by journalists, and she's telling the story of her life. And as she lies, they flash back to what it was really like. They showed me in this slum with my mother, stealing things. Then I said I went to finishing school, and the finishing school was prison. It was very ingenious, and the quick changes, my God, they were miraculous. I had to keep changing back from a glamorous actress to this poor girl. I got wonderful reviews on that, and I was very proud of myself. It was then that Harold Clurman came back and asked me to join the Group Theatre. He said, "You're a complete Stanislavsky actress," and I said, "Who's Stanislavsky?" I think I did *Tell Me Pretty Maiden* without asking Woods's permission. He still got money from me—fifty percent of my salary—but I don't think this was his production. *Tell Me Pretty Maiden* lasted a few months, but it didn't quite make it. I was very disappointed about that because I loved the plot. But it brought me to the attention of Columbia, and they gave me the part in *Holiday* as Hepburn's sister.

SLIDE: Who selected you for *Holiday*?

NOLAN: It must have been a combination of my agent and [George] Cukor. Cukor always liked stage actresses of course. He must have read my reviews. I was very thrilled to work with George Cukor because he was known to be a very good director to work with women—and was. I felt rather good at the time because I got very good reviews on *Tell Me Pretty Maiden,* and I was feeling very proud of myself. *Holiday* was the first time I'd worked with big stars. I was in the makeup room, and [Katharine] Hepburn came in before we started shooting. She chatted with me and said she was delighted I was in the picture. On the set, she was very professional and very fair to work with. But if she thought somebody was taking a scene away from her, she would demand more and more and more takes. You remember the one scene in the bedroom, in front of the mirrors? It was my scene really, but she wanted more and more and more takes. I think we got up to seventy. It was ridiculous. Finally, the cameraman told me that word came down from above that if she wanted any more takes, there wasn't to be any film in the camera. [Laughs]

SLIDE: What about Cary Grant?

NOLAN: I would have gotten along with Cary Grant, but he wasn't very nice to me for some reason. It wasn't that he took a dislike to me. He had a reputation for picking on certain people, and he'd do tricks to make you uncomfortable and upset your performance. That's fair game in the movie business. A lot of them do it. I wasn't very fond of him. He did make me nervous. But the scenes with him came out all right, and I must say he's a very good actor. Personally, I didn't like him.

SLIDE: You shot a scene that is not in the film but was intended as the opening sequence—a scene in the snow.

NOLAN: That's right. Just Grant and I, Cukor, and, of course, the crew. We went up above Lake Arrowhead. Quite high up. I can't remember how long we were there, but we did a lot of scenes in the snow. Then, for some reason, they didn't start the film off with that. It was all cut. I don't know whether they thought I was getting too much footage. It would have taken the surprise from the fact that he [Grant] didn't know my character was rich.

SLIDE: Did you meet Harry Cohn?

NOLAN: Yes. I liked him. I think I had only one interview with him, but he was very affable. I saw him a couple of times after that, and when the film finished, there was a party, at which I talked to him. I remember asking whether I could do a future film there, and he just shook his head and said no. [Laughs] He must have been on his best behavior. He didn't chase me around the office or anything. Nobody ever did in Hollywood. Well, they knew I was going around with Greg [La Cava], so they didn't bother.

SLIDE: *Irene* was a bad career move, in that you are playing, as in *Holiday*, second lead to a woman.

NOLAN: I'll tell you why I did it. My agent was a woman, and she did an awful thing to me. When I was twenty-one—I was underage when I signed the contract with Al Woods—I could have dumped the contract. She said I should re-sign because I had the security of the six months' salary from going back on the stage—which wasn't true. Al Woods was going downhill, and it was a very bad move. I never got out of that contract until I married Alex. I never had any money! Between my agents, publicity people, Al Woods, taxes, it would all disappear. I always lived very modestly. Anyway, I left this agent. Greg said I mustn't stay with her anymore. He thought she was a bad influence on me. Also, maybe, she had too much influence, and he wanted a little control. Myron Selznick was the biggest agent in town. Greg got me in with him, and he got me this second lead in *Irene.* I guess I needed the money, and I wanted to be out on the coast with Greg. That, of course, was a bad career move too.

SLIDE: What were Anna Neagle and Herbert Wilcox like to work with?

NOLAN: They were both very pleasant, but I was being shot only over the back of my neck, and there were close-ups of her all the time. Every time she appeared, they played "In My Sweet Little Alice Blue Gown." I don't think I ever saw the film. I think that was a flop too, and that just about finished me off as far as films were concerned.

SLIDE: You made only two more American films, *Moon Over Burma* and *Follies Girl.*

NOLAN: I've even forgotten the part I played in *Moon Over*

Burma. I don't think I had many scenes with Dorothy Lamour. All I remember were the elephants. There were about six elephants in the film. There had been a fire out at Tarzana on the ranch where they kept the elephants, and some of the elephants had burned ears. The poor things! They were swaying back and forth and moaning. And, of course, the smell from the dirt on the soundstage got to be pretty strong. They had to open the doors and clean it out with shovels.

SLIDE: *Follies Girl?*

NOLAN: Why did I do that rotten film in New York? I think I was just wandering around, out of work, and there was some producer trying to set up a new company. It was shot out on Long Island some place. It might have been Astoria. And they ran out of money and had to stop production in the middle of the thing. I remember [John] Houseman at the time was in New York, and he said, "What the hell are you doing in that film? They haven't got any money. You must be crazy."

SLIDE: Looking back at your screen career, it seems you made one bad career move after another.

NOLAN: That's right. It was bad advice on the part of Woods, who just wanted to make money out of me, and my agent. I was in constant litigation with Woods the whole time. Terrible! I was, naturally, very unhappy. When I got into *Doughgirls*, I was a hit. I began to get offers from Warner Bros., where I should have been in the first place. They did the kind of films that I would have been good in, the meaty, gutsy parts that Bette Davis played. That would have been the perfect studio for me from the beginning. So I flopped in Hollywood, but I was a success on the stage. Let's put it that way.

SLIDE: Now we come to *The Man Who Came to Dinner.*

NOLAN: When I was out in Hollywood, two or three play scripts had been sent to me, and one of them was *The Man Who Came to Dinner.* Greg [La Cava] read the three scripts, and he said, "Take the popular play because it's sure to be a success." So I was signed for the West Coast tour: Los Angeles, San Francisco, Santa Barbara, Seattle. The play was a big hit in New York, with Monty Woolley. Carol Goodner played the part that I eventually played. Edith Atwater always played the secretary, and we became great pals. The play was written about Alexander Woollcott, who was famous for going to visit people and staying in their houses for weeks and months. Woollcott was furious that he hadn't gotten a percentage, and he wanted to make some money out of it. So he said he would like to act in it. He'd never played a big part before. I thought he was medium good. It was Woollcott and Edith, and the chap who played Noel Coward, very, very English, was Rex O'Malley. We all played vignettes that were based on actual people. My part was an international actress, a superficial character but a good actress, who was an American who had gone to England and played there a lot. I based my characterization—slyly—on Gertrude Lawrence.

We opened in Santa Barbara, and, as usual, I didn't do very well because I was nervous. I get into such a state, which is really one of the reasons why theatre and films are such a chore for me. I got these welts on my arms, swelled up about an inch and a half, like big hives. Nerves! We got down to L.A. It was a big opening at the Biltmore, and everybody was there: Hedda Hopper, Louella Parsons, Moss [Hart], and George [S. Kaufman] flew out from New York. W. C. Fields was in the audience. Greg didn't come to the opening night because he was nervous—he came the second night—but Fields called him up and said I was the best thing in the play. I made my entrance, and the audience gasped. I was down to about one hundred twelve pounds. I had long blonde hair, a huge mink coat, a purple dress designed by Hattie Carnegie, a gorgeous hat, and a lot of gold jewelry. I started the scene with Woollcott, and I let out this hysterical laugh. Well, the audience started to laugh, and they laughed for five minutes. We had to just stand there. I hope I'm not bragging too much, but this is actually what happened—and I have to after I flopped in Hollywood! We went up to San Francisco. Warner Bros. came after me, but I had to say no because we were going to Seattle, and it would have been another couple of months before I was free. Then Woollcott had a heart attack after about two weeks. That was the end of that. But, the most wonderful thing in my life happened while I was in San Francisco. [Laurence] Olivier's production of *Romeo and Juliet* with Vivien [Leigh] was on. Olivier had called Alex [Alexander Knox] and asked him to play Friar Lawrence. They were playing in a different theatre from us, different matinees, so I went to see their play and Alex went to see mine. We didn't know each other. Vivien hadn't been very well developed at this point, and you really couldn't hear her beyond the sixth row. The scenery, which was on a turntable thing, was too heavy. Larry had been so busy directing, he hadn't really settled into his part. But after seeing it, I was absolutely struck by Friar Lawrence's performance. It was the best thing in the play, and I went back and told the cast, "There's an absolutely wonderful actor I've never heard of before." A couple of nights later, we went to the Top of the Mark, and their cast and our cast each had a long table for supper. This young, very nice-looking guy stood up, and one of my peers said, "That's Alexander Knox." I said, "Ridiculous, he's an old fart." She said, "No, sometimes he plays older parts."

Their play flopped and mine closed down, and Alex and I both landed in Hollywood. Allan Scott [the screenwriter] was a friend of mine and a friend of Olivier's. Olivier introduced Alex to Allan. Allan and Laura, his wife, introduced me to Alex at their house. It was incestuous. I thought Alex was very nice, but he was a bit reserved. I didn't think he had much of a sense of humor. I guess he was just shy. I thought he was a bit stuffy, but as we got to know each other better, I found out that he had a wonderful, sly sense of humor. Anyway, we started to go out to movies together and have hamburgers and milk shakes. One night we were down at that art cinema, the Coronet on La Cienega, and he informed me he was married. That was a bit of a shock. She was suing for adultery—not with me. His divorce went through, and Laura was determined that we were going to marry. I didn't know this, but this was her plot.

I had broken up with Greg [La Cava] when I was twenty-four years old. At some point, when I was still going around with Greg, I met Alfred Vanderbilt in New York, and I got semi-engaged to him. I went around with him, which got Greg running to New York. [Laughs] I never really fell in love with him, but I liked him very much. We used to go out to Long Island to his mother's house for the weekend, and it was the first time I'd seen how really rich people live. I didn't like the lifestyle. The young society girls were really pretty stupid. They had no intention of doing anything in life. They just wanted to marry a rich man. Like all rich people, Alfred

Vanderbilt was mean. He never carried any money in his pocket. I used to have to pay for taxis. If we had to put petrol in the car, I had to pay for the petrol. His mother broke up that relationship because she didn't want an actress hanging around. And I was fairly bright, and she didn't like that either. [Laughs]

Then I got into *Doughgirls*. It was a silly comedy, but it was fun, and it was a great hit. I shared a flat with Edith [Atwater] at the time, to save money, and then I got my own flat next to her when she married one of her beaus, Hugh Marlowe. That didn't last. They were naughty. He went on tour with Gertrude Lawrence, and God alone knows what was going on there. And Edith was carrying on with somebody else in New York. She went around with Leif Erickson. She went around with George S. Kaufman—and Moss [Hart]! One day, she said to me, "Doris, I'm going out to lunch with Alger Hiss." She was outlandish. She was crazy! Of course, she got blacklisted. She got into a play with Albert Dekker, and she started to go around with him. I don't think he was a Communist. He was just one of those liberals who got it in the neck. Fortunately, Edith had a little bit of income—she came from a well-to-do Chicago family with two flats in New York—and she also ran a prop shop with a friend. After they got blacklisted, she couldn't get any work, so they got together this little program, reading poetry, bits of plays and things, and they went to universities and small theatres.

SLIDE: Were she and Albert Dekker together when he killed himself?

NOLAN: No, he had a wife and children, living in Connecticut.

SLIDE: Everyone claims that Dekker's suicide was connected with his being gay.

NOLAN: He certainly wasn't gay if he was going around with Edith. She wouldn't have put up with it.

SLIDE: At some point around this time, didn't you return to *The Man Who Came to Dinner*?

NOLAN: Oh, I've left out the whole east coast tour of *The Man Who Came to Dinner*. We played the whole eastern seaboard—not New York, because Monty Woolley was still playing it there. We opened in Washington, D.C., at the National Theatre, and the whole cast was invited to the White

House for supper afterwards. Edith and I sat with Woollcott's male secretary and President Roosevelt. We had an absolutely enchanting time. Roosevelt was the most fabulous man I've ever met in my life. He was charming, cheerful, and enjoyed us pretty girls. They couldn't stop his talking, and, of course, Edith and I fell madly in love with him. That was the highlight of our lives.

SLIDE: Was this when George S. Kaufman made a pass at you?

NOLAN: That was earlier on, out in Los Angeles. He used to do this all the time. When he was in New York, he'd been having an affair with Carol Goodner, and he made a pass at Edith [Atwater]. I knew he was going around with Edith. One night, just before I was going on, he came up, took hold of my shoulder, and asked whether I would meet him after the theatre. I said, "Certainly not. Go away. I'm concentrating." I was furious! He really was a horrible man, and, anyway, I didn't find him attractive at all physically. He wasn't my cup of tea. Now where was I?

SLIDE: You were touring.

NOLAN: We went down to Baltimore, and to H. L. Mencken's for supper. Mencken liked pretty girls too, so we had a wonderful time there. We played Philadelphia. One night, Woollcott couldn't get back to New York to record his radio broadcast, so we had the whole studio setup on the stage after the show. They let some of the audience stay. One night in Philadelphia, in a scene with a character called Banjo, who was supposed to be one of the Marx Brothers, a rat ran across the stage. Then, in the next act, there came a line where Banjo says to Sheridan Whiteside, "I smell a rat, a fat rat with spectacles," and of course, the audience fell apart. It was an old theatre in Philadelphia, and there were bats flying around also.

SLIDE: You also appeared in summer stock with *The Man Who Came to Dinner*?

NOLAN: I played it with eight people. I used to go up to Richard Aldrich's summer theatre at Cape Cod, when he was married to Gertie [Lawrence]. I'd been up there before he took it over. I always went up there and played summer stock. Everybody wanted to get in on the act and play *The Man Who Came to Dinner*. Moss [Hart] decided to play it up there. He wasn't too bad. Once in Los Angeles, Woollcott was ill, and [George S.] Kaufman played it. He was terrible. Clifton Webb was the best. He got more laughs than anybody. He was a very precise actor, and hilarious in it. Then I came out to Hollywood at one point, before I was married, and played it with Laird Cregar. He was very good. He was very young, fat but not enormous.

SLIDE: Didn't he kill himself?

NOLAN: Not when I was there. [Laughs] At one point, after the Woollcott tour folded, George [S. Kaufman] asked me to play *The Man Who Came to Dinner* in New York. Carol Goodner had left. I said, "No, I won't take it over. I'm sick of following Carol Goodner around." Anyway, everybody said I was the best one to play it, so I wasn't going to follow anybody else.

SLIDE: After the tour ends, you return to Alexander Knox. In Hollywood?

NOLAN: He'd gone off to Washington. He said I could stay in Hollywood, and he gave me his ration tickets. When he came back, he found out I'd used all his ration tickets, and he was absolutely furious. We had nothing to eat for weeks.

SLIDE: He wasn't drafted?

NOLAN: He was when we were in New York at one point. They turned him down because he had ulcers, and also because of his age. He did do intelligence work in Canada, propaganda to get the United States into the war. He did do his bit.

SLIDE: When did he propose to you?

NOLAN: I'm trying to remember. I never remember important things. Gradually, I guess, we decided to get married. We lived like a family with the Scotts, Allan and Laura, Pippa and David [the two children], and we went down to Mexico together. We had a civil ceremony at Allan Scott's house. Barry Fitzgerald was the best man, and Edith Atwater was the maid of honor.

SLIDE: What was the date?

NOLAN: December 30, 1944. I married two men that night! Barry had the ring and was fumbling with it. Judge Mosk said, "With this ring, I thee wed." And Barry finally got the ring and stuck it on my finger. Mosk was just about to say, "I now pronounce you man and wife." Aagh! We had to start all over again. I'd married the wrong man. We took the ring off, started again, and got properly married.

SLIDE: Did you have a honeymoon?

NOLAN: We lived at Sunset Towers at the time, a big apartment building on Sunset Boulevard. Laura and Allan used to rent a beach place every summer at Del Monte, and we went there. Oh, I know what happened! The day after we married, Moss Hart called me from New York, and he wanted me to go out and entertain the troops in the Pacific. I said, "Oh, what an adventure this will be. I can't wait to go." Alex said, "You're not going. If you go, I won't be here when you come back." That was that. I was furious. I had hysterics. I told him I was sorry I married him, that he was a terrible man, too bossy. We had a fine row. Anyway, I soon got over that.

SLIDE: Didn't Alex and Barry Fitzgerald ride around on motorbikes together?

NOLAN: I stopped that.

SLIDE: I can't imagine either of them on motorbikes. Was it their hobby?

NOLAN: It didn't go that far. They used to go tearing around at ninety miles an hour up in the Hollywood Hills, and they used to take pistols with ammonia in them and shoot at the dogs that would attack them. The studio didn't want him to ride his motorbike anyway. Barry and I were very good friends. He was a darling man. I went to visit him in Ireland just before he died. Mimi, the wife of Wells Root [the screenwriter], and I went over. He was dying of a brain tumor, and I must say he looked awful. He had a very good friend, a newspaper publisher, who took care of him. He stayed with Barry out in Hollywood for a while, and so he took care of him in Dublin when he was ill.

SLIDE: Your career peters out at this point. Did Alex ask you not to work?

NOLAN: Like all men, he said, "Take it easy for a while." They always want you to themselves! That's when the rumor went around that I was going to retire, which I had no intention whatsoever of doing. Nothing came along for a while, and then I had a child, Andrew. We moved to a biggish house, with a lot of steps, in Laurel Canyon. I learned to cook and do the social thing. Alex turned down two films, which upset me. He

turned down *Les Miserables* because he said Fredric March had
been so good in it [the 1935 version], and he didn't think it was
such a good idea to do it so soon after that. I think it was a
mistake, careerwise, to turn down those films. He should have
done exactly what [Darryl F.] Zanuck wanted. Zanuck was
crazy about him in *Wilson*. He said it was one of the greatest
film performances he had ever seen.

SLIDE: Your friends were generally left wing?

NOLAN: Liberals. We used to know Julie [John] Garfield,
Vincent Price, the Lloyds [Norman and Peggy]. Sol Kaplan and
Fra [his wife] were very good friends of ours. Kirk Douglas lived
up the street from us. We met a lot of writers through Allan
Scott: John Wexler, John Paxton, Philip Dunne, and, of course,
Adrian Scott. John Houseman was a very close friend. George
Colouris. John Huston. Dorothy Parker came to the house a
couple of times, and we used to see her at nightclubs.

SLIDE: Were you aware that the political climate was changing?

NOLAN: Yes. I remember the day Andrew was born, Alex
was off at a political meeting with Phil Dunne and John Huston.
It was so complicated. The first thing was the CSU [Conference
of Studio Unions] strike. Alex and Franchot Tone and
[Katharine] Hepburn tried to get the screen actors to picket the
studios and support this little union. The gangsters were
beating up the union organizers. Alex spoke at a big meeting at
the Screen Actors Guild, about whether we were going to join
the strike. Ronald Reagan was the president of the Screen Actors Guild at that time. William Holden was at the meeting, I
remember, and he was always pretty right wing. [Roy] Brewer
was at the meeting. A Communist, Waldo Salt, helped Alex
write the script. What Alex did was to make fun of telephone
negotiations. He imitated Ronnie [Reagan] doing these telephone conversations with the gangsters in Chicago. You know
how Ronnie used to talk: blah, blah, blah, blah, blah. They had a
sort of prizefighter's ring, and all the actors, hundreds of them,
were sitting around. Alex got up and he started to imitate
Ronnie, and the audience was absolutely hysterical. The audience began to laugh so at Alex's imitation that these goons
came from the back of the arena. They had canes and were hitting the seats, marching down the aisles, and they were going

to beat Alex to a pulp. I've never been so frightened in my life. They were almost to the platform, and Franchot [Tone] got up and said to Alex, "You must stop." He wasn't allowed to finish his speech, but Franchot Tone got it all quieted down. Alex walked off the platform that night, and Brewer said to him, "You son of a bitch, I'm going to run you out of town." We would have won the meeting that night, but they did a postal vote, and we lost. Of course, at that time, we didn't realize Ronald Reagan was an FBI informant, peaching on all of us liberals.

SLIDE: At what point did you start worrying about your careers?

NOLAN: Alex was always interested in politics. I was just a Roosevelt voter. I'd sign things, the way we all did, but I would have been too timid to be very active politically. I didn't realize how terribly interested he was getting in all this. Like a fool, he put the Committee for the First Amendment's phone in our house. I really raised the roof about that because I realized it wasn't a good thing for him to do, he being a Canadian. I kept warning him he was going to get into trouble because he wasn't an American.

About this time, Alex had written a play called *The Closing Door*, a melodrama. It was very stark and gloomy, but quite good. Alex had written parts for him and me, and we would costar. Jed Harris wanted to do it, but Alex didn't get along with him. He took it to producer Cheryl Crawford, and [Elia] Kazan liked it very much and was going to direct it. He dumped us because he got a film, and Cheryl suggested that we get Lee Strasberg. We didn't know too much about Lee at that point, but we'd heard small things about him and we weren't very keen about the idea. Cheryl insisted. He obviously needed a job, and he was one of the boys. I thought he was a poseur. He had no talent. He was a publicity seeker. He ruined a lot of actors' careers, made them nervous wrecks, and I think the people who became successful became successful despite him. He and his wife had a terrible effect on Marilyn Monroe. Like Stella Adler, we thought he was just Mister No Talent, and he ruined the play. Allan Scott said he had never seen a thing directed so badly in his life. We went out of town, up to Boston, and Alex kept rewriting and improving. We tried his changes out at the matinee, and put them in at the evening performance. We were about to open in two weeks in New York, and Lee hadn't even gotten around to setting up the third act of the play. He used to sit around and talk all the time. The first two days of rehearsals he sat down and explained the play to Alex and me. An absolute waste of time. We knew what the play was about! When we finally opened in New York [1949], Lee hadn't finished some of the technical details. He was just impossible. Awful! Finally, he and Alex weren't speaking, and Lee would just sit there. He didn't even come to the opening night. We got respectable reviews, and it went on to be a success on television after we had left the United States. Cheryl brought Lillian Hellman to see it the opening night. We had supper with her at the Algonquin afterwards, and she thought it was about three-quarters good. She was a terrific woman. But Lee ruined it, and I'll never forgive him. At that point in our careers, it would have been a very good thing. It would have made a big difference. Things were very bad politically by then. People were testifying.

SLIDE: Why weren't you or Alex subpoenaed?

NOLAN: They only subpoenaed the ones they knew were Communists, and they knew we weren't Communists. You were graylisted or blacklisted. We were so-called graylisted. Alex hated the Communists. He hated any dogmatic thing, like the Catholic Church or communism.

SLIDE: What happened next?

NOLAN: Benn Levy [the playwright] called from London and wanted Alex to do this play called *Return to Tyassi* with his wife, Connie [Constance Cummings]. Tyrone Guthrie was directing. Alex had played with Benn and Connie before, and he said he'd like to do it. I think he was a little bit anxious to get out of Hollywood. He said, "You and the child come along because otherwise I don't think I'll stay there." We packed, closed up the house, and off we went to London. I'd never been to England before.

SLIDE: Did you know then that you were never going back to America?

NOLAN: Oh no. I don't think I would have gone had I thought that. Alex knew trouble was brewing, but I don't think he realized we would stay in England for the rest of our lives. Anyway, he had started his career in England, and he was glad to get back.

SLIDE: How did the move affect you personally?

NOLAN: How do you know in this business how long a play is going to run, what's going to happen? People had begun to travel all over the world on location. I was used to him going off. There was no food in England then—1950—and you saw the effects of the bombing all over England. The food was revolting. You'd get a little packet of gray flour and two eggs a month. I sent some money to a friend in New York and got food parcels.

SLIDE: When did it become apparent that you were going to settle here?

NOLAN: It took a long time. The play, unfortunately, only ran for six weeks at the Duke of York's Theatre. It got good reviews, but it just didn't go. It was 1951, and we rented a house above Kensington High Street, which was very nice. It had five stories, and Alex had his study on the top floor. I seem to get into steps all the time. [The original home Doris and Alex inhabited in Berwick-upon-Tweed was four stories, with the living room and kitchen on the third floor. Her present home in Berwick is a second and third floor apartment.] We were down at the Festival of Britain [on the South Bank of the river Thames in 1951] with Andrew, and we ran into Ingrid Bergman. She was with [Roberto] Rossellini at the time, and they were in England trying to set up a film. Nothing would do but that Alex would come to Rome and do the film, which was great. In the meantime, his agent had phoned from Hollywood and said he had a picture at Columbia with Loretta Young [*Paula*, 1952]. He went back and did that, and it was at that time the American Legion got after him. They marched up and down in front of the Pantages Theatre [in Hollywood], saying Alex and Sidney Buchman, who was a writer at Columbia at the time, were Communists. Alex said to Harry Cohn, "I've got to sue. I can't let them go around saying I'm a Communist." Harry Cohn said, "No, don't sue. It will clear up. It will only make a lot of bad publicity."

SLIDE: Of course Loretta Young was very right wing.

NOLAN: Oh very. But she knew he wasn't a Communist. [Andre] de Toth wanted him for that Western [*Man in the*

Saddle, 1951]. His business manager said, "I think you'd better make some more money. While you're here, do it."

We had to be in Rome at a certain time, so while he was doing the second picture, I packed up the house and drove to Rome. Alex came, and we started the film with Ingrid and Rossellini. It was called *Europa '51* [also known as *The Greatest Love*, 1954]. He played her husband, and she was playing another of those slightly saintly St. Joan roles. She was fixated on St. Joan. Rossellini had a funny way of shooting. He wouldn't shoot in the morning, so he'd start say twelve or one o'clock in the afternoon and shoot through to about eight or nine at night. He was pretty disorganized. He wasn't a very organized person. Every time Rossellini felt like it, he'd take us off to his summer place up the coast, and we'd have lovely lunches and swim. He loved Italy, and he loved to show people around. There wasn't any script particularly. He had a young Negro American writer on it, and people on the film speaking five different languages. He also used some contessas and friends of his, playing parts, not professional actors. I think Ingrid was pregnant at that time, and the Catholic Church was trying to get them married. She was in a state because her husband in America wouldn't let her talk to Pia, her daughter. He'd taken all of her money, the house, everything. He was a real swine to her. They finally got through the film. I've forgotten how long they took to shoot, but I remember going down in hot weather and I think we were there over the winter. At one point, Connie and Benn came over. We had an allowance in lire, and also, this is very important, Alex's business manager in the United States, Lewis Deak, had arranged for Alex to be paid in three separate segments, in American dollars. They made a deposit of one-third before he started the film. In the middle of the film, they made the second deposit. As it happened, we never got the third amount. Lew called up and said, "Don't finish the film because the money hasn't come in." Unfortunately, he'd finished the film the day before.

Connie and Benn wanted him to come back and do a new play of Benn's. Don't ask me the name of the play. We opened in Glasgow, which I thought was so depressing. There was trouble from the beginning. Benn had trouble with the director. Alex didn't quite understand his part. He kept asking Benn whether he was supposed to be a virgin or not. [Laughs] They folded and never came into London. So we went back to London, and Connie had rented us a house with five stories in South Kensington. I just always seem to be running up and down stairs. It's the story of my life. I could call my life *Stepping Stones.*

When we were still in Rome, Lew Deak called and said to Alex, "You can't come back to the United States. You're in trouble politically. If you come back, you'll land on Ellis Island, and they'll deport you." He said, "Just cool it and stay in England." Alex's agent at the time was MCA, and he was signed up to play in *The End of the Affair* [1954], costarring Deborah Kerr and Van Johnson. They didn't sign a contract because it was a verbal thing with the agency. He would have been given a contract later. He was fitted with his wardrobe. Three days before he started the film, word came from New York that he was unacceptable for the part. We didn't dare think it was political. Why would they have bothered to try and do something to us in England? Alex had said he would stay and work in England and that nobody would bother him here. A few days later, the agency had gotten the information that he was politically unacceptable. That meant he was going to be blacklisted in England. Anyway, he was supposed to get a big hunk of money for the film. The contract hadn't been signed, but Alex said, "I'll sue and I'll win, because everyone [at the agency] can testify for me." A verbal contract was a holy thing with an agency. An executive, whose name I will not mention [Lew Wasserman], said, "I'm sorry, but nobody in my office is going to testify for you." Didn't get a cent, was blacklisted, and lost a film. That meant he wasn't going to make any more films with American money, no matter where. That meant seven years before he made another film with any American money in it. Alex did get into one British film after another. Naturally, a lot of the time, he didn't get the billing or the money. But he kept busy. I did quite a bit of television—didn't get much money.

SLIDE: When did you start working in British television?

NOLAN: As soon as possible. I did one play, *Who's Afraid of Virginia Woolf?* Connie [Cummings] played the original British production. I just played it at the Liverpool Playhouse and on a tour of Wales. I decided after that experience never to work on the stage again. The whole thing was a disaster. The young girl in the company was smoking pot, and she was difficult to direct. The director wasn't very good. The leading man went into diabetic comas. What with one thing and another, we had a great time! When we got to Wales, they were so shocked by the play, they used to throw things at us, and talk back to us.

SLIDE: You always played American women on television?

NOLAN: Always. I had one big success on television. The BBC did a film about the shooting of Kennedy, an all-American cast. I had one scene where I had to describe the killing of Kennedy. It was a long, hysterical scene, and I thought, Oh great, I'm going to have a great career at the BBC. I never got anything good again.

SLIDE: You mentioned a couple of series you were in, *The Adventures of Robin Hood* and *Colonel March of Scotland Yard.*

NOLAN: They were backed by the American Communists. Dalton Trumbo had put money in and set up [producer] Hannah Weinstein. She was a friend of Dashiel Hammett, and he put up money as well. They had all these high-priced writers, and Americans shipped them over. It was a Communist organization. I don't think Howard Koch was a Communist, but he came over.

SLIDE: Were these recurring roles or cameos?

NOLAN: Just cameos. I did only three or four of them.

SLIDE: Did Alex do any?

NOLAN: He did one with me, but it wasn't one of those. It wasn't fancy enough for him. You know what she was paying us? I think I used to get twenty-five dollars a day. Carl Foreman and Joe Losey always hired us. Alex worked with Joe a lot. The first one they did together was *The Sleeping Tiger* [1954]. I was in *The Servant* and *The Romantic Englishwoman.*

SLIDE: What was Losey like as a director?

NOLAN: We always got along fine. A lot of people didn't get along with him. He was very gloomy on the set. He didn't seem to have much of a sense of humor, but he had wonderful taste. Joe had a very good eye with the camera, and his films always looked wonderful. He didn't have much story sense. He was lucky to get [Harold] Pinter. He had great trouble finishing *The Romantic Englishwoman.*

SLIDE: You were in the last scenes in the film. Were they shot last?

NOLAN: I think in the middle. I just happened to see it a couple of years ago, and the ending was a mess. I think they went back and reshot it.

SLIDE: You were not concerned that you were playing such small parts?

NOLAN: I didn't give a damn. I knew that I wouldn't get anywhere. There was too much competition around. I didn't have a chance here because Irene Worth was here, and Connie [Constance Cummings]. Benn was always writing plays for Connie. So there were two big American actresses. I got interested in antiques and opened this antique gallery. Anyway, I'd lost interest in acting. Alex said I was put off because I'd landed in such a nest of vipers when I was young. They all took advantage of me—leeches—and they were all living off my back. It just got to be too much for me.

SLIDE: In all published filmographies, *Isadora* is listed as one of your films.

NOLAN: No, I wasn't in that. I'm quite sure.

SLIDE: You were in the Richard Lester film *Juggernaut* [1974].

NOLAN: We had a wonderful time because we shot it all on a Russian cruise ship. The Russians had bought it from the Germans after the war. It was a fighting ship that had been transformed into a cruise ship. This was the maiden voyage, and the producers hired the whole ship on which to film nine-tenths of the film. It was a blackmail thing about somebody threatening to blow up the ship if the ransom money wasn't paid. Richard Harris was the man who comes on board and defuses the bomb. Anthony Hopkins was in it, but he wasn't on the ship. I got my son a small part in it. What they did was to take all the leading actors on board, and they picked up a lot of extras in Southampton. They just paid them a little bit, expenses, and got them to fill up the ship. It was a very pleasant cruise until we got to the Orkneys. The scene was supposed to be shot on very rough seas, but the waves weren't big enough. So they took the stabilizers off without telling anybody, and the ship began to rock. That's when three-quarters of the people got seasick.

SLIDE: So when did you retire?

NOLAN: Retire? I never decided. Actors never decide when they're going to retire. It just happens. Work stops coming. Andrew got a scholarship to Cambridge, and he went off. I started my antique gallery. We skidded along on money. We never starved, but we were never very rich. It was because Alex had started his career in England that he was able to make a second career here. We were goddam lucky. We could have starved to death in America. We always pretended that nothing had happened to us politically. Alex thought it would be bad for his career if it was known he was blacklisted. Adrian Scott came over and lived near us. He got a contract at M-G-M for a while, but he didn't do well. Finally, the one who broke the blacklist for Alex as far as American money in Europe was concerned was Kirk Douglas. He put him in *The Vikings* [1958] with Tony Curtis, and that had United Artists money in it. I made a film in Denmark with Walter Shenson [*Welcome to the Club*, 1971]. Alex made a film in Denmark [*Hidden Fear*, 1957]. He gave up the stage because as he got older, it was much too hard for him. But he kept doing television. He did *Tinker, Tailor, Soldier, Spy,* and we got a promotional trip to New York. For the first time in twenty-five years, he went back to the States. I remember, he went up to the American Consulate in Edinburgh because he was nervous about going back. He wanted to be sure that he was clear. Nervously, he kept asking, "Can you look and see whether there is any record about me?" She looked at him as if he were crazy and said, "No, I can't find anything."

SLIDE: After that trip to New York, neither of you wanted to return to America?

NOLAN: No. He hated America. After what they'd done, wouldn't you? No. We'd settled here forever. That was the only trip back he ever made.

Doris Nolan died in Berwick-upon-Tweed on July 29, 1998.

Phil Brown and Donna Reed in *Calling Dr. Gillespie* (1942).

Phil Brown (fourth from left) in *H. M. Pulham, Esq.* (1941).

Phil Brown in *The Hidden Room/Obsession* (1949).
Courtesy of British Film Institute.

Rose Hobart during filming of *Liliom* (1930).

Mildred Van Dorn, Rose Hobart, Charles Farrell, and
Estelle Taylor in *Liliom* (1930).

Halliwell Hobbes, Fredric March, and Rose Hobart in
Dr. Jekyll and Mr. Hyde (1932).

Marsha Hunt relaxes on the set of *Smash-Up* (1947).

A posed portrait of Marsha Hunt and Alexander Knox in
None Shall Escape (1944).

Marsha Hunt in *None Shall Escape* (1944).

Marsha Hunt, Margaret Sullavan, and Ann Sothern in
Cry "Havoc" (1943).

A recent photograph of Marsha Hunt.

Marc Lawrence, Dick Curtis, Robert Warwick, and
Mary Russell in *Squadron of Honor* (1938).

Victor McLaglen and Marc Lawrence in
The Princess and the Pirate (1944).

A recent photograph of Marc Lawrence.

Doris Nolan.

Doris Nolan and John Boles in *As Good as Married* (1937).

Jack Carr, Doris Nolan, and John Litel in
One Hour to Live (1939).

Doris Nolan (third from left) on stage with Alexander Woollcott
in *The Man Who Came to Dinner* (1940).

Doris Nolan in *Holiday* (1938).

Doris Nolan and Alexander Knox on stage in
The Closing Door (1949).

A Rebuttal

ALEXANDER KNOX RESPONDS TO CHARGES THAT HE IS A MEMBER OF THE COMMUNIST PARTY

Blacklisted or graylisted actors and actresses were forced to defend themselves in many ways against charges of being members of the Communist Party. The following letter was written by Alexander Knox to Roy Brewer in February 1954, at the suggestion of Philip Dunne. It was Dunne who provided Knox with the list of points to which to respond, noting that Numbers 1, 3, 4, 5, 8, 10, and 11 were the most serious accusations. As Knox's business manager, Lewis J. Deak, explained to the actor (in a letter dated April 9, 1954),

> I personally had a talk with Mr. Brewer and also with Mike Luddy, who is a personal attorney and a friend of Brewer's, and a member of the law firm of Bodkin, Breslin & Luddy. Apparently the way the thing works is as follows: your letter is submitted by Brewer, to whom it was addressed, to a committee consisting of individuals from the unions, Screen Actors Guild and the producers. If, in the opinion of this group, the writer has justified himself, they then either individually or collectively let it be known to all the studios that you have sent a letter in and that you have justified your position, and as far as anyone is concerned you are eligible for employment without any criticism.

Rereading the letter in later years, Knox commented,

> Many parts of this letter I hate. It's a weasel-letter in intention. I don't think I was as mealy-mouthed as the letter suggests. The curious and interesting thing is that the letter didn't work. I had no offers of work in American pictures until five years later.

The letter is reprinted exactly as written by Knox, from a carbon copy preserved in his files, except that typographical errors have been corrected.

Dear Mr. Brewer:

Some time ago I was given to understand that one of the major studios in Hollywood wanted me for a part in a film I was interested in doing, but, a few weeks later, I was told that the studio would not employ me because I was suspected of being a member of the Communist Party. Although this suspicion is fantastic and utterly without foundation I received a list of incidents and organizations which, taken at their face value, might tend to justify the suspicion. This letter is an effort to discuss the list and to explain, as far as possible, my attitude towards the various items on it. I trust you will give my explanation your sympathetic consideration. I have always enjoyed my visits to Hollywood and I have depended on them for a certain part of my livelihood. I should not like to feel that they had been made impossible either by unfounded suspicions or a failure to express my opinions clearly.

I had the pleasure of meeting you on one occasion: when you were invited by the Board of the Screen Actors Guild to express the point of view of the Union of which you were the leader. I spoke also on that occasion, and, while our views were at variance, it was my impression that you did your duty sincerely and well by the organization of which you were the head. My hope is that you will believe that my attitude was no less sincere, and based on what I conceived to be my duty to the S.A.G. [Screen Actors Guild]. Certainly I am confident that you will not allow your special interests on that occasion, or our divergence of opinion, to prejudice your consideration of the material in this letter.

The following is a list of points on which, I understand, an explanation is felt to be required.

1   6-30-45—*PW* p. 4: Protested Gerald L. K. Smith at HISCAP meeting.

2   9-3-46—[*The*] *Hollywood Reporter*: One of sponsors of a dinner forum given by *The Nation* Associates 9-22-46 at Ambassador Hotel. Forum Topic: "The Challenge of the Post War World and the Liberal Movement."

3   12-20-46—*LA Daily News*: Signer of petition for meeting of Screen Actors Guild to review their general strike policy.

4   11-20-46—*PW* p. 2: Will appear at home of Craig Rice at a meeting under auspices of Thomas Jefferson Bookshop.

5   7-5-47—*PW* p. 5: To participate in actors panel, "Thought Control," sponsored by Hollywood PCA.

6   10-22-47—*LA Daily News*: Expressed disgust and outrage at testimony in Washington Red Hunt Investigation, in full-page trade paper ad.

7   2-20-48—*LA Examiner*: At current Tenney Committee hearings Ira Gershwin said he had hosted a meeting of the Committee for the First Amendment, 10-15-47, which subject attended.

8   1945: Peoples' Educational Centre fall term booklet says Knox will be chairman of a course for the layman.

9   1945: Actors' Lab program of "An Evening at the Lab." lists Knox as audience sponsor.

10   Oct. '51 *Alert* p. 7: Active in Screen Writers Guild. Endorsed Lester Cole and Ring Lardner, Jr., as candidates for exec. board of S.W.G. in Nov., 1948.

11   9-11-45: Photostat of P.E.C. circular says Knox will be chairman of a new series of film forums sponsored by P.E.C. course.

I shall deal with these points in order.

1   6-30-45—*PW* p. 4: Protested Gerald L. K. Smith at HISCAP meeting.

To the best of my recollection I was never a member of HISCAP, nor was I sympathetic to all the activities of this organization. I must confess, however, that, while I do not remember the occasion mentioned, I have for many years disapproved of the anti-semitic activities of Smith, and if those activities were the basis of the "protest" the probability is that I should have supported it.

2   9-3-46—*[The] Hollywood Reporter*: One of the sponsors of a dinner forum given by *The Nation* Associates 9-22-46 at Ambassador Hotel. Forum topic: "The Challenge of the Post War World and the Liberal Movement."

I remember this meeting well. I have subscribed to *The Nation* for some years although I do not by any means agree automatically with its editorial position. The meeting was widely attended by eminent people in Hollywood. The chief speaker was, I believe, Thurman Arnold, and I was glad to hear his address. As he and *The Nation* have been anti-communist for many years I do not understand how my presence at this meeting can be interpreted as evidence of communist affiliations or sympathies. Thurman Arnold and *The Nation* have both been the subject of attack by communist and fellow-travellers on countless occasions.

3   12-20-46—*LA Daily News*: Signer of petition for meeting of Screen Actors Guild to review their general strike policy.

I not only signed the petition but, with Miss [Katharine] Hepburn, [Dame] May Whitty and others I discussed the contents and I spoke at the meeting. It was on that occasion that I met you, and I should like to recall to your mind a couple of incidents which occurred. I asked you privately if you thought such meetings in a Guild or Union did any good. (You will recollect that representatives from all the organizations involved were invited to speak.) You replied that you were glad to have the opportunity of re-stating the I.A.T.S.E. position but that, as a help to settling the dispute, you believed such meetings to be worse than useless and referred me to the section of your speech where you suggested that the meeting was communist-inspired. There was not time then to continue the discussion and this seems to be a suitable opportunity to present my point of view. It is, of course, somewhat delayed, and my memory is by no means infallible, but my opinions at that time were, I think, somewhat as follows:

I was, of course, aware that the communists in the S.A.G. would support the meeting and the resolution that was passed. My interest was a very simple one and by no means coincided with the interests of the communists. I had never been aware of such disunity in the S.A.G. We faced difficult negotiations at that time. There were many voices in Guild affairs urging that the Guild refuse to cross picket lines. Some members did so refuse. It was my belief that the Guild might easily split on the issue. It was my further belief that the only way to prevent more trouble in the Guild was to reunite on the stated official policy of the Guild—neutrality. A neutrality, incidentally, that encouraged the actors to cross the C.S.U. [Conference of Studio Unions] picket lines. It seemed to me that the Board of Directors of the S.A.G. was moving too rapidly away from this policy and towards an open support of the I.A.T.S.E. position.

You were, of course, only doing your duty in your efforts to gain the support of the S.A.G. for the I.A.T.S.E. I thought it my duty at the time to oppose any move away from the position of neutrality which the S.A.G. had adopted. There were loud voices calling "Let us refuse to cross picket lines!" and there were louder voices calling "Let's help smash the C.S.U.!" In my opinion neither of these positions was apt to be helpful to the S.A.G. After all a split is a split, whether it be even or uneven. The policy of neutrality had the overwhelming support of the membership. A move in either direction at that time would, in my opinion, have meant trouble, disunity and a loss of strength. Many members of the Board of Directors with whom I discussed the matter—even some who felt that the C.S.U. position was subversive and hopeless—agreed with me that the subject should be aired. The majority of the Board felt that it had already been discussed. Since I disagreed with this majority I had the right, and duty, as a member to petition for a meeting. As far more than the necessary number of signatures was obtained on the petition within forty-eight hours I have no doubt that the meeting fulfilled a real need in the Guild.

You may remember the further course of events in the S.A.G. A resolution along the general lines of policy I favored gained the support of the meeting. It was sent out on referendum. The membership rejected it.

Those who wished to disrupt the Guild continued to agitate for a refusal to cross picket lines. It was a simple matter to point to the meeting and the referendum as evidence that the subject had, once again, been fairly discussed and that the membership had spoken fully and decisively.

In my opinion it would have been infinitely preferable if the Board of Directors had called the meeting without the stimulus of the petition; but, as events turned out, the danger of disruption in the Guild decreased since it was now possible to make a clear distinction between those who accepted the decision of the majority and those who did not.

It is possible I was wrong in the whole affair. Certainly some members of the Board of Directors, if I can accept hearsay evidence, took the opportunity to misread my motives. Equally certainly my actions were not communist-inspired. I was always aware of the potential disruption from the Left. I believe still that the holding of this meeting lessened the danger of disruption. The whole series of events is, in my opinion, an example of the proper working of the democratic method. The one thing it is not is precisely what some members of the Board of Directors thought it was—an example of how communist-inspired activity in a union can be stopped. If the Board of Directors had called the meeting themselves they could adopt that position. They did not call the meeting. And now a few of those who did call the meeting have since been vilified for precisely the disruptive action which, by calling the meeting, they succeeded in preventing. It is for such purposes that democratic freedoms are necessary and it is when they are not used, not when they are used, that Democracy fails.

4   11-20-46—*PW* p. 2: Will appear at the home of Craig Rice at meeting held under auspices of Thomas Jefferson Bookshop.

Although I recollect the name Craig Rice, I do not remember in what connection. [Craig Rice was a prominent mystery writer, the pseudonym of Georgiana Ann Randolph.] To the best of my belief I have never entered the Thomas Jefferson Bookshop. Certainly I have no idea where it is, or why I should attend a meeting under its "auspices."

5   7-5-47—*PW* p. 5: To participate in actors panel, "Thought Control," sponsored by Hollywood PCA.

I recollect vaguely some meeting, I think at a Beverly Hills hotel, which I attended for an hour one evening and left early. It is possible that this is the actors panel referred to. If it is, and if I lent my name to it, which I consider doubtful, I can say quite definitely that I took part in no "Panel" on that occasion.

6   10-22-47—*LA Daily News*: Expressed disgust and outrage at testimony in Washington Red Hunt Investigation, in full-page trade paper ad.

I do not recollect having signed any trade paper ad on this matter. If someone to whom the appropriate files of trade papers are available would be kind enough to look up the issues involved I am confident that my recollection will be proved correct. [The advertisement in question appeared on October 28, 1947, and Alexander Knox's name is not present.]

7   2-20-48—*LA Examiner*: At current Tenney Committee hearings Ira Gershwin said he had hosted a meeting of the Committee for the First Amendment, 10-25-47, which subject attended.

I attended several meetings of the Committee for the First Amendment, and I presume Mr. Gershwin is correct in his recollection. Is the Committee for the First Amendment now considered a "Communist Front" organization? That was certainly not my impression at the time. Communists, or people who consistently followed the communist line were not prominent in any of the deliberations I attended. There was, if I remember rightly, a deliberate policy of exclusion.

The communist position in 1947 involved the following two propositions—

1. — That the Congressional Committee had no legal or moral (?) right to investigate.

2. — That the ten "unfriendly witnesses" were legally and morally (?) justified in refusing to testify.

The Committee for the First Amendment, on the other hand, took the view that the Congressional Committee had not only the right but the duty to investigate; and that the "unfriendly ten" were doing a typical disservice to Democracy in refusing to testify. These were the opinions of the members of the Committee for the First Amendment with whom I came in contact. I should be very surprised to learn that any official statement of the Committee expressed a different view.

But, to go farther, the only meeting of the Committee which I remember with clarity took place after the hearings in Washington, when the Committee was disbanding. At this meeting a group of the "unfriendly ten" presented their case to the Committee for the First Amendment and I remember in some detail the efforts of that Committee to persuade the ten to alter their position and to agree to testify even at that late date. I also remember the vituperation to which the members of the Committee were then subjected. Apparently the Committee is now the subject of vituperation from quite different sources.

The general purpose of the Committee for the First Amendment, as I understood it, was to protest against the manner of the Congressional Hearings. It is still my opinion that the manner is as important as the matter. There is an old judicial aphorism that runs something like this—"It is not enough that justice be done, justice must be seen to be done." I should like to point out the great difference between the conduct of the hearings in 1947 under Congressman [J. Parnell] Thomas and the trials of the communists before Judge [Harold R.] Medina. The recordings of the hearings under Congressman Thomas are still used assiduously in Italy, France, Canada and the United Kingdom in an effort to stimulate anti-American feeling. It is not hard to guess what party uses these recordings; nor is it hard to judge their effect, especially in countries like Italy and France which have felt on their own soil the results of the same disregard for human rights. The conduct of Congressional hearings has, in general, improved greatly during the past seven years; but the weapons which Congressman Thomas gave gratis to the enemies of democracy are still being used. Not a few of the present difficulties of Mr. [John Foster] Dulles in Europe are directly traceable to the stunned and shocked amazement with which democratic Europeans listened to the reckless murder of reputation, the utter disregard of legal safeguards and the Moscow-style vituperation permitted and indulged in by Congressman Thomas at those hearings in 1947.

In spite of the widespread disgust and outrage expressed at the time by many prominent individuals, organizations and newspapers, including the *New York Herald Tribune*, the Committee for the First Amendment never denied the right of Congress to investigate, and many members spent much time and energy trying to persuade the "unfriendly ten" to reverse their uncooperative stand. I should not be giving a true picture of my political convictions, however, if I failed to say that, in my opinion, Democracy is in grave danger from many procedures which verge on being extra-legal. No matter how the communist may exacerbate and twist the democratic process, a healthy society defeats him by argument, not suppression. For this the communist must, of course, be recognized as such. He cannot be so recognized unless he is invited to express himself in an atmosphere of freedom. I believe that a democratic society is in greater danger from a communist grimacing from a hole in the ground—somewhere under the platform—than from a communist invited to stand on the platform where he will be forced by public opinion to exercise his right and duty to express himself sincerely—if he can.

It was a feeling of ignorance and an over-scrupulous regard for the legal issues involved which persuaded me against signing the official statements of the First Amendment Committee—not any lack of sympathy with its deep concern for the rights of free expression. [In reality, Alexander Knox was not a signer of the original statement of the Committee for the First Amendment because he was not an American citizen.] The whole question of the investigation of opinion is a complex one. I believe that membership in the Communist Party is sufficient grounds for the firing of an employee from any position where national security is involved. I am not convinced that it is wise to carry the ban into the area of less sensitive or civilian employment since the danger to civil liberties may well out-weigh the possible advantages of a public opinion artificially united by such methods. Democracy is not necessarily easier to preserve when it has destroyed the foundation on which it rests.

You can, I am sure, understand my doubt since the process of the investigation of thought has now widened to include me. Hence this letter. I happen to know that I am innocent of any subversive act or intention, but, as far as employment goes, I am guilty until I can prove myself innocent. That might be difficult enough if there were a court before which I might plead, a court with all the delicate controls, safeguards and rules of evidence which form an important part of the heritage of the West, the chief protection of our way of life and the chief distinguishing mark of our courts as opposed to the "courts" of the communists.

But I have no court to which I can appeal. No court, no lawyer, no jury, no trained judge. In this effort I can depend upon two factors only—my ability to convince, and the fairness of a group of men whom I do not know and who, by the very nature of the circumstances, must be assumed to disagree with me on many profound matters. My accusers are my judges.

You may be interested to know my attitude towards the fear of communism in the United States—which Harry Truman described as a "Red Herring"—before I received from my agents the stunning allegation of "unreliability." On many occasions I expressed the following opinions in the United States and abroad: that action against communists was affecting only communists; that the Communist Party in the U.S.A. was disruptive in the extreme; that it used Democracy to subvert Democracy; that the evidence of such action was, in my opinion, conclusive; and, finally, that the propaganda line suggesting that innocent people were being involved was grossly misleading and unsupported by any evidence that had come my way.

Now that I have been "involved" in a manner which necessitates this letter what should my attitude be?

8   1945: Peoples' Educational Centre fall term booklet says Knox will be chairman of a course for the layman.

For consideration of this item see section 11, which deals with the same occasion.

9   1945: Actors' Lab program of "An Evening at the Lab." lists Knox as audience sponsor.

I do not recollect sponsoring programs at the Lab. although I recollect giving two lectures there, which may have been on this occasion. My consenting to lecture there may very naturally have been considered sufficient authorization to describe me as a "sponsor." The theme of one lecture was the usefulness to actors of training in classical drama. The occasion was connected with a production of Ben Johnson's *Volpone*, the sixteenth century morality, which the Lab. presented with real imagination. The other lecture I remember was a general one on English drama from Shakespeare to Shaw. The Lab. was one of the few theatres operating in Los Angeles in 1945 which consistently tried for quality in performance and direction. I was pleased when I observed any tendency there to do plays of proven merit. This tendency was not always pronounced in Los Angeles and when it did show itself I felt it my duty to encourage it. The general policy of the Lab. did not encourage me to join it, nor do I think that my lectures were very popular as I was not invited again, but whenever I am given an opportunity to present a case for the classic drama I am glad to do so before any audience that will listen. Lectures at U.S.C. and U.C.L.A. were more frequent than at the Lab., at least partly because my point of view is more acceptable at a university than at the Lab. I have lectured on drama in many States of the Union, in Canada and in England, before groups of farmers, Government Departments, Roman Catholics, Methodists, and teachers. I have lectured at the Old Vic, at Boston University. I have directed and advocated religious drama before the General Assembly of the United Church of Canada. I have visited drama festivals in many parts of Canada and officially opened the Dominion Festival, founded by Lord Bessborough when he was governor general of the Dominion. The classic theatre is one of my consuming interests, and I have always been glad when I have been invited to appear again at the Old Vic, where I received valuable training many years ago. My last appearance there was on the occasion of the Coronation production of *Henry VIII* in which I played Cardinal Wolsey and had the pleasure of being presented again to Her Majesty and the Duke of Edinburgh. I mention this, not because it is pertinent in itself, but because I gave up a profitable New York engagement to appear there, and should be glad to do so again. This seems to me to prove, to some extent at least, that my interest in the Classic drama is considerably greater than my interest in the Actors Lab. or any similar organization. When such an organization, however, shows an interest in the fundamental history and tradition of the theatre I must say that I feel very strongly that such interest should be cultivated. I am only sorry that I failed to persuade anyone at the Actors Lab. to take a more liberal attitude to the drama.

10   Oct. '51 *Alert* p. 7: Active in the Screen Writers Guild. Endorsed Lester Cole and Ring Lardner, Jr., as candidates for exec. board of S.W.G. in Nov., 1948.

To deal with the last part of this item—it would be foolish to discuss or try to explain it as I have not the faintest recollection of the occasion. If it could be recalled to me and I could understand precisely what is meant by "endorsed" in this connection it is possible I might remember special circumstances which could explain an attitude which I certainly do not hold now and which I find it very hard to believe that I held then.

As for being active in S.W.G. affairs in 1951, it is my belief that I was not even an active member in that year. I was an active member for very few years. I left Hollywood in 1949 to do my own play at the Empire Theatre, New York, and in 1950 I did a play at the Duke of York's Theatre in London. I returned to Hollywood for a period of seven or eight weeks in March and April 1951, and again for a period of six weeks, September into October, the same year. The rest of that year was spent in Canada, in Italy and in England. Incidentally, I wrote only two films in Hollywood, *Sister Kenny* for Rosalind Russell at RKO and *The Judge Steps Out* for Ann Sothern and myself at the same studio. I never considered myself well enough acquainted with S.W.G. affairs to take an "active" part at any time.

11   (also see Section 8) 9-11-45: Photostat of P.E.C. circular says Knox will be chairman of a new series of film forums sponsored by P.E.C. course.

I did agree to conduct a series of film forums once a week for four months. I did this in the same spirit and from the same point of view that I lectured at the Lab. The results were similar. At the first two meetings I remember speaker after speaker uttering cliches about social significance which had nothing to do with the technique of the film or the subject under discussion. My efforts to bring the discussion back to the subject were listened to respectfully but elicited no response from the floor. I decided I needed some help, so I asked Mr. Charles Coburn to accompany me to the next meeting, which he did. He was very popular and we had a certain amount of lively discussion on the film in question which was, I believe, one Mr. Coburn had played a part in. I was pleased at the result and set to work to line up some other interesting actors to help in the discussion. If I remember correctly I had acceptances from Barry Fitzgerald, May Whitty and a few others who knew their profession. Unfortunately, the series was cancelled after the third meeting. I presume that I failed to conduct the forum in a manner acceptable to the authorities. I was not sorry, really, because I found it very difficult to maintain my interest in a group that preferred to consider a strip of film purely as a political document instead of as a story in words and pictures.

That is the last item on the list of incidents and organizations which I received as requiring explanation. Now for a few general remarks on the whole subject of "reliability."

I have never been a communist. I have never been invited to

become a member, probably because I never hesitated to express my opinion of the party's dangerous totalitarian tendencies. I have felt the danger of these tendencies since my university days and my feeling was reinforced and intensified by, among others, three incidents which occurred to me in the late twenties and early thirties. Although these incidents may seem to be off the subject I should like to enlarge on them briefly in the hope that the stories may help you to get a clear picture of my political thinking.

Through the Sunday Editor of the *Boston Post*, a paper for which I worked during 1929, I became acquainted with the aggressive and exacerbationist tendencies of the Communist Party during the police strike in Boston while Calvin Coolidge was Governor of Massachusetts. In the early thirties I returned for a while to London, Ontario, where a long-continued and distressing printers' strike helped to bring about the collapse of the powerful Liberal daily, *The London Advertiser*. (The Liberal Party in Canada corresponds roughly to the Democratic Party in the U.S.A.) I had worked for *The London Advertiser* off and on over a period of many years and I knew many members of the staff. Through them I had a fairly direct knowledge of the disruptive part played by the Communist Party in this strike.

A year or so later I recall a meeting in London, England, while I was appearing in an Edgar Wallace play at Wyndham's [Theatre]. The meeting was addressed by George Lansbury on his return from a visit to Russia. It was a time when many visitors to the Soviet Union returned full of enthusiasm—partly because Russia was outspoken against events and tendencies in Italy and Germany. I was sceptical of this Russian enthusiasm, even when expressed by such observers as Sydney and Beatrice Webb.

At this particular meeting an incident occurred which seems to me very dramatic. George Lansbury followed Lady Astor, I believe, and spoke enthusiastically of many things he had seen in Russia. Towards the end of his speech an elderly woman interrupted Lansbury with some authority. I was told she was Emma Goldman, the anarchist. She asked Lansbury if he had seen the prisons in Moscow and Leningrad. He said he had.

"Even the Lubianka?" asked Emma Goldman.

"Yes," said Lansbury.

"That was where I was imprisoned."

"You were imprisoned everywhere."

"Did you talk to any of the prisoners in the Lubianka?"

"I did," said Lansbury.

"Did you talk to a man with only one side to his face, short, with graying red hair?" asked Emma Goldman.

"Yes, I talked with him for some time."

"Did he tell you why he was in prison?"

"No. I understood he was there for a short sentence."

"He has now been sent to Siberia," said Emma Goldman, and continued "Do you know why he was imprisoned?"

"No. I didn't ask."

"He was imprisoned for translating and printing one of your speeches, George," and Emma Goldman sat down.

I recall the incident vividly, and I mention it in an effort to make clear to you the social and political convictions I actually hold, and have held, as opposed to the convictions some people have evidently tried to ascribe to me—ascriptions which have made this letter necessary. It was the Emma Goldman incident which dramatized for me my existing scepticism regarding the propaganda of the Soviet Union. I have seen or heard nothing since to persuade me to modify that scepticism.

In this connection, may I point out that I am a writer as well as an actor, that I have had four novels published and two plays performed in New York and London, that I have contributed many articles to papers as diverse as the *Boston Post* and the *Times Literary Supplement*. It is interesting to me, and necessary, to find out what is going on. I have frequently found myself in company I should have preferred to do without—I once spent two weeks reporting an international Morticians' Convention, but that did not make me a mortician.

I presume the main question is the valid one of how I, with my opinions, could allow myself to associate with organizations or groups in which communists were involved. My reasons are, basically, three.

First: The communist line of propaganda has attracted many people. They can be prevented from accepting it by one of two methods—fear or persuasion. I know no item in the communist dogma which cannot be refuted quite conclusively in fair and open discussion. Force was employed for two decades in Italy and for five years in France. As a direct result these countries are plagued and torn apart by the most powerful communist parties in Europe.

Second: If a Democrat refuses to associate at any point with a communist, or to support any issue which the Communist Party happens at the moment to support—in other words, if my actions are to be rigidly governed in a negative sense by Communist Party tactics; if I must wait, on any issue, to see what line the Communist Party plans to take and then do the opposite—the Communist Party is left freely to choose the area of battle and can build a vast following on the basis of popular and liberal policies in which they do not for a moment sincerely believe. That is what has happened in France and what has, most notably, not happened in the United Kingdom. The United Kingdom is probably the only power of any military consequence in the world outside the U.S.A. and Turkey which can and does face the possibility of war with Russia without fear of domestic crisis. The United Kingdom bears the heaviest per capita arms burden in the West, maintains the longest term of required military training in the West, and is actively engaging communists on three battlefields today without relaxing the ancient regard in which civil liberties are held.

Third: I believe that the legitimate desire of many patriotic citizens of the United States to counteract the dangerous influence of the Communist Party has taken a form which is unlikely, in the long run, to achieve this result. Vigilance, certainly; fear, never. I believe that a Democracy with the traditions of the United States is in much greater danger from the fear of communism than from communism itself. I find myself in the position of having to write this letter precisely because of that fear. I have not the slightest objection to expressing my views to anyone who may be interested, nor do I feel the need to hold any of my thoughts in reserve, and I am sure you can understand my beliefs even though you may not sympathize with all of them. You can see that I must find it strange and rather shocking suddenly to discover that I am suspected of communist sympathies when it is precisely the totalitarian type of organization, of which the Communist Party is the best example, to which I have most strenuously objected all my adult life.

Membership in the Communist Party is, of course, sufficient basis for any government to dismiss a man from any position where he might conceivably endanger security. But the extension of this practice to areas of civil employment is, I believe, dangerous. Force or blacklists are not necessary where thought is vigilant and argument is free. The fantastic switches in direction thought necessary in the Communist Party, culminating before the last war in the Hitler Stalin pact, were themselves sufficient in an era of relative freedom from the fear of communism to disgust many former adherents. It is necessary for Democracy to call pointed attention to these lies and inconsistencies. If the Party is muzzled the lies are whispered, not spoken in public, and so cannot be shown for what they are. The result is a dangerous secret movement, peopled by neurotic and power-mad zealots whose most powerful weapon is precisely the secrecy into which they are forced. The Democrat can always deal with the enemy he can see.

I believe, for instance, that the communist parties in both Italy and France are less powerful today than they were at the end of the war. Under Mussolini and Petain they gained in strength. Under a Democratic regime they are losing it. Communist parties function well in an atmosphere of repression. Why shouldn't they? It is the atmosphere they invariably create when they obtain power, and it is the only atmosphere they fully understand. I believe it can be accepted almost as an axiom that the degree of danger from internal communist parties varies inversely with the degree of Democratic freedom.

To conclude this long letter—and its length is largely due to my desire to give as complete a picture of my political beliefs as possible, a thing not easy to do in capsule form—I want to say that I am fully aware that a great many Americans, possibly a majority, would disagree with most of my conclusions at the present time. They would hold that more rigorous methods than I believe in are necessary and that I am visionary and impractical. It may be that I am, but there is no doubt that those who may differ from me in opinion hold a power over my livelihood which I should not like to hold over the livelihood of anyone. I have described my beliefs as they are without concealment or equivocation for the purpose of enabling you to understand them as fully as possible. I believe most profoundly in the Democratic method. I believe it is the duty as well as the privilege of a Democrat to be prepared to state his beliefs honestly and fully. My sincere hope is that this belief in Democracy, and the efforts I have made in this letter and elsewhere to act on a basis of this belief in Democracy, will not persuade anyone that I am unfit to earn my living in a Democracy.

It may be thought that I am naive, an easy dupe for communists. But who has never been duped by them? The man who could truly say that he had never, during the past thirty years, been fooled by communists must be either a very unhappy or a very evil man. I certainly have been so fooled but the occasions grew fewer as I grew older and more prudent.

In spite of this growth of prudence it is still my belief that the "naive" and Christian faith that has inspired six generations of my people, North and South of the 49th parallel, to help build this continent in freedom is more valuable to me as a heritage and a rule of life than all the prudence in the world. It is faith, not doubt, that moves mountains; it is faith, not fear, that makes the leper whole, and it was St. Francis, not Torquemada, who was proud to call himself the Fool of God.

FILMOGRAPHIES

Phil Brown

I Wanted Wings (Paramount, 1941). Director: Mitchell Leisen. With Ray Milland, William Holden, and Wayne Morris. As Masters.

H. M. Pulham, Esq. (M-G-M, 1941). Director: King Vidor. With Hedy Lamarr, Robert Young, and Ruth Hussey. As Joe Bingham.

Pierre of the Plains (M-G-M, 1942). Director: George B. Seitz. With John Carroll, Ruth Hussey, and Bruce Cabot. As Val Denton.

Calling Dr. Gillespie (M-G-M, 1942). Director: Harold S. Bucquet. With Lionel Barrymore, Philip Dorn, and Donna Reed. As Roy Todwell.

Hello, Annapolis (Columbia, 1942). Director: Charles Barton. With Tom Brown, Jean Parker, and Larry Parks. As Kansas City.

Weird Woman (Universal, 1944). Director: Reginald Le Borg. With Lon Chaney Jr., Anne Gwynne, and Evelyn Ankers. As David Jennings.

The Impatient Years (Columbia, 1944). Director: Irving Cummings. With Jean Arthur, Lee Bowman, and Charles Coburn. As Henry Fairchild.

Jungle Captive (Columbia, 1945). Director: Harold Young. With Otto Kruger, Amelita Ward, and Jerome Cowan. As Don Young.

Over 21 (Columbia, 1945). Director: Charles M. Vidor. With Irene Dunne, Alexander Knox, and Charles Coburn. As Frank MacDougal.

State Fair (20th Century-Fox, 1945). Director: Walter Lang. With Jeanne Crain, Dana Andrews, and Dick Haymes. As Harry Ware.

Without Reservations (RKO, 1946). Director: Mervyn LeRoy. With Claudette Colbert, John Wayne, and Don DeFore. As soldier.

The Killers (Universal, 1946). Director: Robert Siodmak. With Burt Lancaster, Ava Gardner, and Edmond O'Brien. As Nick.

Johnny O'Clock (Columbia, 1947). Director: Robert Rossen. With Dick Powell, Evelyn Keyes, and Lee J. Cobb. As hotel clerk.

If You Knew Susie (RKO, 1948). Director: Gordon M. Douglas. With Eddie Cantor, Joan Davis, and Allyn Joslyn. As Joe Collins.

The Luck of the Irish (20th Century-Fox, 1948). Director: Henry Koster. With Tyrone Power, Anne Baxter, and Cecil Kellaway. As Higginbotham.

Moonrise (20th Century-Fox, 1948). Director: Frank Borzage. With Dane Clark, Gail Russell, and Ethel Barrymore. As Elmer.

Obsession (Independent Sovereign, 1949). Director: Edward Dmytryk. With Robert Newton, Sally Gray, and Naunton Wayne. As Bill Kronin. Released in the United States as *The Hidden Room*.

Give Us This Day (Plantaganet, 1949). Director: Edward Dmytryk. With Sam Wanamaker, Lea Padovani, and Kathleen Ryan. Assistant director. Released in the United States as *Salt to the Devil*.

No Sad Songs for Me (Columbia, 1950). Director: Rudolph Mate. With Margaret Sullavan, Wendell Corey, and Viveca Lindfors. Dialogue director.

The Harlem Globetrotters (Columbia, 1951). Director: Phil Brown. With Thomas Gomez, Dorothy Dandridge, and Bill Walker.

The Green Scarf (B&A/British Lion, 1954). Director: George More O'Ferrall. With Michael Redgrave, Leo Genn, and Ann Todd. As John Bell.

A King in New York (Attica/Archway, 1957). Director: Charlie Chaplin. With Charlie Chaplin, Dawn Adams, and Oliver Johnston. As headmaster.

The Camp on Blood Island (Hammer/Columbia, 1958). Director:

Val Guest. With Andre Morell, Carl Mohner, and Barbara Shelley. As Lieutenant Bellamy.

John Paul Jones (Samuel Bronston/Warner Bros., 1959). Director: John Farrow. With Robert Stack, Marisa Pavan, and Charles Coburn. As sentry.

The Counterfeit Stranger (Perlberg-Seaton/Paramount, 1962). Director: George Seaton. With William Holden, Lilli Palmer, and Hugh Griffith. As Harold Murray.

The Bedford Incident (Bedford/Columbia, 1965). Director: James B. Harris. With Richard Widmark, Sidney Poitier, and James MacArthur. As CMM McKinley.

The Boy Cried Murder (Carlos-Avala-Bernard Luber/Universal, 1966). Director: George Breakston. With Veronica Hurst, Fraser MacIntosh, and Tim Barrett. As Tom.

The Adding Machine (Associated London/Universal, 1969). Director: Jerome Epstein. With Phyllis Diller, Milo O'Shea, and Billie Whitelaw. As Ben.

Land Raiders (Charles H. Schneer/Columbia, 1969). Director: Nathan Juran. With Telly Savalas, George Maharis, and Arlene Dahl. As Mayfield.

Operation Cross Eagles (Noble-Triglav/Continental, 1969). Director: Richard Conte and Casey Diamond. With Richard Conte, Rory Calhoun, and Aili King. As Sergeant Tunley. Filmed in Yugoslavia under original title of *Unakrsna Vatra*.

Tropic of Cancer (Joseph Strick/Paramount, 1970). Director: Joseph Strick. With Rip Torn, James Callahan, and Ellen Burstyn. As Van Norden.

Valdez Is Coming (Ira Steiner/United Artists, 1971). Director: Edwin Shein. With Burt Lancaster, Susan Clark, and Jon Cypher. As Malson.

Scalawag (Bryna/Paramount, 1973). Director: Kirk Douglas. With Kirk Douglas, Mark Lester, and Neville Brand. As Sandy.

The Romantic Englishwoman (Dial/Meric-Matalon/New World, 1975). Director: Joseph Losey. With Glenda Jackson, Michael Caine, and Helmut Berger. As Wilson.

The Pink Panther Strikes Again (Amjo/United Artists, 1976). Director: Blake Edwards. With Peter Sellers, Herbert Lom, and Colin Blakely. As the senator.

Get Charlie Tully (T.B.S. Distributing, 1976). Director: Cliff Owen. With Dick Emery, Darren Nesbitt, and Ronald Fraser. As an American.

Star Wars (20th Century-Fox, 1977). Director: George Lucas. With Mark Hamill, Harrison Ford, and Carrie Fisher. As Uncle Owen Lars.

Twilight's Last Gleaming (Lorimar-Bavaria-Geria/Allied Artists, 1977). Director: Robert Aldrich. With Burt Lancaster, Richard Widmark, and Charles Durning. As Reverend Cartwright.

Silver Bears (Raleigh/Columbia, 1978). Director: Ivan Passer. With Michael Caine, Cybill Shepherd, and Louis Jourdan. As a banker.

Superman (Dovesmead/Warner Bros., 1978). Director: Richard Donner. With Marlon Brando, Gene Hackman, and Christopher Reeve. As the state senator.

Rose Hobart

Liliom (Fox, 1930). Director: Frank Borzage. With Charles Farrell, Estelle Taylor, and Lee Tracy. As Julie.

A Lady Surrenders (Universal, 1930). Director: John M. Stahl. With Conrad Nagel, Genevieve Tobin, and Basil Rathbone. As Isabel Bravel.

Chances (Warner Bros., 1931). Director: Allan Dwan. With Douglas Fairbanks Jr., Anthony Bushell, and Mary Forbes. As Molly Prescott.

East of Borneo (Universal, 1931). Director: George Melford. With Charles Bickford, Georges Renavent, and Lupita Tovar. As Linda Randolph.

Compromised (Warner Bros., 1931). Director: John G. Adolphi. With Ben Lyon, Claude Gillingwater, and Juliette Compton. As Ann.

Dr. Jekyll and Mr. Hyde (Paramount, 1931). Director: Rouben Mamoulian. With Fredric March, Miriam Hopkins, and Holmes Herbert. As Muriel Carew.

Scandal for Sale (Universal, 1932). Director: Russell Mack. With Charles Bickford, Pat O'Brien, and Claudia Dell. As Claire Strong.

The Shadow Laughs (Trojan/Invincible, 1933). Director: Arthur Hoerl. With Hal Skelly, Harry T. Morey, and Robert Keith. As Ruth Hackett.

Convention Girl (Falcon/First Division, 1935). Director: Luther Reed. With Robert Weldon Heyburn, Sally O'Neil, and Herbert Rawlinson. As Babe Laval.

Tower of London (Universal, 1939). Director: Rowland V. Lee. With Basil Rathbone, Boris Karloff, and Barbara O'Neil. As Anne Neville.

Wolf of New York (Republic, 1940). Director: William McGann. With Edmund Lowe, James Stephenson, and Jerome Cowan. As Peggy Nolan.

Susan and God (M-G-M, 1940). Director: George Cukor. With Joan Crawford, Fredric March, and Ruth Hussey. As Irene Burrows.

A Night at Earl Carroll's (Paramount, 1940). Director: Kurt Neumann. With Ken Murray, Blanche Stewart, and J. Carroll Naish. As Ramona Lisa.

Ziegfeld Girl (M-G-M, 1941). Director: Robert Z. Leonard. With James Stewart, Hedy Lamarr, and Judy Garland. As Mrs. Merton.

Singapore Woman (Warner Bros., 1941). Director: Jean Negulesco. With Brenda Marshall, David Bruce, and Virginia Field. As Alice North.

Lady Be Good (M-G-M, 1941). Director: Norman Z. McLeod. With Eleanor Powell, Ann Sothern, and Robert Young. As Mrs. Carter Wardley.

Nothing But the Truth (Paramount, 1941). Director: Elliott Nugent. With Bob Hope, Paulette Goddard, and Edward Arnold. As Mrs. Donnelly.

I'll Sell My Life (Select Attractions, 1941). Director: Elmer Clifton. With Michael Whalen, Stanley Fields, and Joan Woodbury. As Dale Layden.

No Hands on the Clock (Pine-Thomas/Paramount, 1941). Director: Frank McDonald. With Chester Morris, Jean Parker, and Dick Purcell. As Mrs. West.

Mr. and Mrs. North (M-G-M, 1941). Director: Robert B. Sinclair. With Gracie Allen, Paul Kelly, and Virginia Grey. As Carol Brent.

A Gentleman at Heart (20th Century-Fox, 1942). Director: Ray McCarey. With Cesar Romero, Carole Landis, and Milton Berle. As Claire Barrington.

Who Is Hope Schuyler? (20th Century-Fox, 1942). Director: Thomas V. Loring. With Joseph Allen Jr., Mary Howard, and Sheila Ryan. As Alma Pearce.

Prison Girls (PRC, 1942). Director: William Beaudine. With Sidney Blackmer, Claire Rochelle, and Lynn Starr. As Rosemary Walsh.

Dr. Gillespie's New Assistant (M-G-M, 1942). Director: Willis Goldbeck. With Lionel Barrymore, Van Johnson, and Susan Peters. As Mrs. Black.

Salute to the Marines (M-G-M, 1943). Director: S. Sylvan Simon. With Wallace Beery, Fay Bainter, and Reginal Owen. As Mrs. Carson.

Swing Shift Maisie (M-G-M, 1943). Director: Norman Z. McLeod. With Ann Sothern, James Craig, and Jean Rogers. As inspector on the assembly line.

The Adventures of Smilin' Jack (Universal, 1943). Directors: Ray Taylor and Lewis D. Collins. With Tom Brown, Marjorie Lord, and Philip Ahn. As Fraulein Von Teufel. A twelve-chapter serial.

The Mad Ghoul (Universal, 1943). Director: James Hogan. With David Bruce, Evelyn Ankers, and George Zucco. As Della.

Crime Doctor's Strangest Case (Columbia, 1943). Director: Eugene J. Forde. With Warner Baxter, Lynn Merrick, and Lloyd Bridges. As Mrs. Burns.

Song of the Open Road (Charles R. Rogers/United Artists, 1944). Director: S. Sylvan Simon. With W. C. Fields, Jane Powell, and Bonita Granville. As Mrs. Powell.

The Soul of a Monster (Columbia, 1944). Director: Will Jason. With George Macready, Jim Bannon, and Jeanne Bates. As Lilyan Gregg.

The Brighton Strangler (RKO, 1945). Director: Max Nosseck. With John Loder, June Duprez, and Michael St. Angel. As Dorothy.

Conflict (Warner Bros., 1945). Director: Curtis Bernhardt. With Humphrey Bogart, Alexis Smith, and Sydney Greenstreet. As Kathryn Mason.

The Cat Creeps (Universal, 1946). Director: Erle C. Kenton. With Noah Beery Jr., Lois Collier, and Paul Kelly. As Connie Palmer.

Canyon Passage (Universal, 1946). Director: Jacques Tourneur. With Dana Andrews, Susan Hayward, and Brian Donlevy. As Marta Lestrade.

Claudia and David (20th Century-Fox, 1946). Director: Walter Lang. With Robert Young, Dorothy McGuire, and Mary Astor. As Edith Dexter.

The Farmer's Daughter (RKO, 1947). Director: H. C. Potter. With Loretta Young, Joseph Cotten, and Ethel Barrymore. As Virginia.

The Trouble with Women (Paramount, 1947). Director: Sidney Lanfield. With Ray Milland, Teresa Wright, and Brian Donlevy. As Dean Agnes Meeler.

Cass Timberlane (M-G-M, 1947). Director: George Sidney. With Spencer Tracy, Lana Turner, and Zachary Scott. As Diantha Marl.

Mickey (Eagle-Lion, 1948). Director: Ralph Murphy. With Lois Butler, Bill Goodwin, and Irene Hervey. As Lydia Matthews.

Bride of Vengeance (Paramount, 1949). Director: Mitchell Leisen. With Paulette Goddard, John Lund, and Macdonald Carey. As Eleonora.

Marsha Hunt

The Virginia Judge (Paramount, 1935). Director: Edward Sedgwick. With Walter C. Kelly, Stepin Fetchit, and Johnny Downs. As Mary Lee Calvert.

Desert Gold (Paramount, 1936). Director: James Hogan. With Larry "Buster" Crabbe, Monte Blue, and Glenn Erikson. As Judith Belding.

Gentle Julia (20th Century-Fox, 1936). Director: John G. Blystone. With Jane Withers, Tom Brown, and Jackie Searl. As Julia Atwater.

The Arizona Raiders (Paramount, 1936). Director: James Hogan. With Larry "Buster" Crabbe, Raymond Hatton, and Jane Rhodes. As Harriett Lindsay.

Hollywood Boulevard (Paramount, 1936). Director: Robert Florey. With John Halliday, Robert Cummings, and C. Henry Gordon. As Patricia Blakeford.

The Accusing Finger (Paramount, 1936). Director: James Hogan. With Paul Kelly, Kent Taylor, and Robert Cummings. As Claire Patterson.

Easy to Take (Paramount, 1936). Director: Glenn Tryon. With John Howard, Eugene Pallette, and Richard Carle. As Donna Westlake.

College Holiday (Paramount, 1936). Director: Frank Tuttle. With Jack Benny, George Burns, Gracie Allen, and Mary Boland. As Sylvia Smith.

Murder Goes to College (Paramount, 1937). Director: Charles F. Riesner. With Roscoe Karns, Lynne Overman, and Larry "Buster" Crabbe. As Nora Barry.

Easy Living (Paramount, 1937). Director: Mitchell Leisen. With Jean Arthur, Edward Arnold, and Esther Dale. As unbilled woman at film's close.

Annapolis Salute (Paramount, 1937). Director: Christy Cabanne. With James Ellison, Harry Carey, and Van Heflin. As Julia Clemens.

Thunder Trail (Paramount, 1937). Director: Charles Barton. With Gilbert Roland, Charles Bickford, and J. Carroll Naish. As Amy Morgan.

Born to the West (Paramount, 1937). Director: Charles Barton. With John Wayne, John Mack Brown, and John Patterson. As Judy Worstall.

Come on, Leathernecks (Republic, 1938). Director: James Cruze. With Richard Cromwell, Leon Ames, and Edward Brophy. As Valerie Taylor.

The Long Shot (Fine Arts/Grand National, 1939). Director: Charles Lamont. With Gordon Jones, C. Henry Gordon, and George Meeker. As Martha Sharon.

Star Reporter (Crescent Pictures/Monogram, 1939). Director: Howard Bretherton. With Warren Hull, Morgan Wallace, and Clay Clement. As Barbara Burnette.

The Hardys Ride High (M-G-M, 1939). Director: George B. Seitz. With Lewis Stone, Mickey Rooney, and Fay Holden. As Susan Bowen.

Winter Carnival (Walter Wanger/United Artists, 1939). Director: Charles F. Riesner. With Ann Sheridan, Richard Carlson, and Helen Parrish. As Lucy Morgan.

These Glamor Girls (M-G-M, 1939). Director: S. Sylvan Simon. With Lew Ayres, Lana Turner, and Tom Brown. As Betty Ainsbrudge.

Joe and Ethel Turp Call on the President (M-G-M, 1939). Director: Robert B. Sinclair. With Ann Sothern, Lewis Stone, and Walter Brennan. As Kitty Crusper.

Irene (RKO, 1940). Director: Herbert Wilcox. With Anna Neagle, Ray Milland, and Roland Young. As Eleanor Worth.

Pride and Prejudice (M-G-M, 1940). Director: Robert Z. Leonard. With Greer Garson, Laurence Olivier, and Mary Boland. As Mary Bennet.

Ellery Queen, Master Detective (Larry Darmour/Columbia, 1940). Director: Kurt Neumann. With Ralph Bellamy, Margaret Lindsay, and Charles Grapewin. As Barbara Brown.

Flight Command (M-G-M, 1940). Director: Frank Borzage. With Robert Taylor, Ruth Hussey, and Walter Pidgeon. As Claire.

The Trial of Mary Dugan (M-G-M, 1941). Director: Norman Z. McLeod. With Robert Young, Laraine Day, and Tom Conway. As Agatha Hall.

Cheers for Miss Bishop (Richard A. Rowland/United Artists, 1941). Director: Tay Garnett. With William Gargan, Edmund Gwenn, and Sterling Holloway. As Hope Thompson.

The Penalty (M-G-M, 1941). Director: Harold S. Bucquet. With Edward Arnold, Lionel Barrymore, and Robert Sterling. As Katherine Logan.

I'll Wait for You (M-G-M, 1941). Director: Robert B. Sinclair. With Robert Sterling, Virginia Weidler, and Paul Kelly. As Pauline Miller.

Blossoms in the Dust (M-G-M, 1941). Director: Mervyn LeRoy. With Greer Garson, Walter Pidgeon, and Felix Bressart. As Charlotte.

Unholy Partners (M-G-M, 1941). Director: Mervyn LeRoy. With Edward G. Robinson, Edward Arnold, and Laraine Day. As Gail Fenton.

Joe Smith, American (M-G-M, 1942). Director: Richard Thorpe. With Robert Young, Harvey Stephens, and Darryl Hickman. As Mary Smith.

Kid Glove Killer (M-G-M, 1942). Director: Fred Zimmermann. With Van Heflin, Lee Bowman, and Samuel S. Hinds. As Jane Mitchell.

Panama Hattie (M-G-M, 1942). Director: Norman Z. McLeod. With Red Skelton, Ann Sothern, and Rags Ragland. As Leila Tree.

Seven Sweethearts (M-G-M, 1942). Director: Frank Borzage. With Kathryn Grayson, Van Heflin, and Cecilia Parker. As Regina.

Thousands Cheer (M-G-M, 1943). Director: George Sidney. With Mickey Rooney, Judy Garland, and Red Skelton. As a prospective Wave.

Lost Angel (M-G-M, 1943). Director: Roy Rowland. With Margaret O'Brien, James Craig, and Philip Merivale. As Katie Mallory.

The Human Comedy (M-G-M, 1943). Director: Clarence Brown. With Mickey Rooney, Frank Morgan, and James Craig. As Diana Steed.

Pilot No. 5 (M-G-M, 1943). Director: George Sidney. With Franchot Tone, Gene Kelly, and Van Johnson. As Freddie.

Cry "Havoc" (M-G-M, 1943). Director: Richard Thorpe. With Margaret Sullavan, Ann Sothern, and Joan Blondell. As Flo Norris.

None Shall Escape (Columbia, 1944). Director: Andre de Toth. With Alexander Knox, Henry Travers, and Erik Rolf. As Marja Pacierkowska.

Bride by Mistake (RKO, 1944). Director: Edward Wallace. With Alan Marshall, Laraine Day, and Allyn Joslyn. As Sylvia.

Music for Millions (M-G-M, 1944). Director: Henry Koster. With Margaret O'Brien, Jose Iturbi, and June Allyson. As Rosalind.

The Valley of Decision (M-G-M, 1945). Director: Tay Garnett. With Greer Garson, Gregory Peck, and Donald Crisp. As Constance Scott.

A Letter for Evie (M-G-M, 1946). Director: Jules Dassin. With John Carroll, Hume Cronyn, and Spring Byington. As Evie O'Connor.

Smash-Up, The Story of a Woman (Walter Wanger/Universal-International, 1947). Director: Stuart Heisler. With Susan Hayward, Lee Bowman, and Eddie Albert. As Martha Gray.

Carnegie Hall (Federal Films/United Artists, 1947). Director: Edgar G. Ulmer. With William Prince, Frank McHugh, and Martha O'Driscoll. As Nora Ryan.

Raw Deal (Eagle-Lion/Reliance, 1948). Director: Anthony

Mann. With Dennis O'Keefe, Claire Trevor, and John Ireland. As Ann Martin.

The Inside Story (Republic, 1948). Director: Allan Dwan. With William Lundigan, Charles Winninger, and Gail Patrick. As Francine Taylor.

Take One False Step (Chester Erskine/Universal-International, 1949). Director: Chester Erskine. With William Powell, Shelley Winters, and James Gleason. As Martha Wier.

Jigsaw (Tower/United Artists, 1949). Director: Fletcher Markle. With Franchot Tone, Jean Wallace, and Myron McCormick. As unbilled cameo.

Mary Ryan, Detective (Columbia, 1949). Director: Abby Berlin. With John Litel, June Vincent, and Harry Shannon. As Mary Ryan.

Actors and Sin (Benjamin B. Smith/United Artists, 1952). Director: Ben Hecht. With Edward G. Robinson, Dan O'Herlihy, and Rudolph Anders. As Marcia Tillayou.

The Happy Time (Columbia, 1952). Director: Richard Fleischer. With Charles Boyer, Louis Jourdan, and Linda Christian. As Susan Bonnard.

Diplomatic Passport (Rich & Rich-Princess/Eros, 1954). Director: Gene Martel. With Paul Carpenter, Henry Oscar, and Honor Blackman. As Judy Anderson.

No Place to Hide (Josef Shaftel/Allied Artists, 1956). Director: Josef Shaftel. With David Brian, Hugh Corcoran, and Ike Jariego Jr. As Anne Dobson.

Bombers B-52 (Warner Bros., 1957). Director: Gordon Douglas. With Karl Malden, Natalie Wood, and Efrem Zimbalist Jr. As Edith Brennan.

Back from the Dead (Regal Films/20th Century-Fox, 1957). Director: Charles Marquis Warren. With Peggie Castle, Arthur Franz, and Don Haggerty. As Katy.

Blue Denim (20th Century-Fox, 1959). Director: Philip Dunne. With Carol Lynley, Brandon de Wilde, and Macdonald Carey. As Jessie Bartley.

The Plunderers (Joseph Pevney/Allied Artists, 1960). Director: Joseph Pevney. With Jeff Chandler, John Saxon, and Dolores Hart. As Kate Miller.

Johnny Got His Gun (Bruce Campbell Productions, 1971). Director: Dalton Trumbo. With Jason Robards, Timothy Bottoms, and Diane Varsi. As Johnny's mother.

Rich and Famous (M-G-M, 1981). Director: George Cukor. With Jacqueline Bisset, Candice Bergen, and David Selby. As Malibu party guest.

MARC LAWRENCE

If I Had a Million (Paramount, 1932). Directors: Ernst Lubitsch, Norman Taurog, Stephen Roberts, Norman Z. McLeod, James Cruze, and William Seiter. With Gary Cooper, Charles Laughton, and George Raft. As a hood.

Gambling Ship (Paramount, 1933). Directors: Louis Gasnier and Max Marcin. With Cary Grant, Benita Hume, and Jack La Rue. Unbilled.

White Woman (Paramount, 1933). Director: Stuart Walker. With Carole Lombard, Charles Laughton, and Charles Bickford. As Connors.

Death on the Diamond (M-G-M, 1934). Director: Edward Sedgwick. With Robert Young, Madge Evans, and Nat Pendleton. Unbilled.

Million Dollar Baby (Monogram, 1934). Director: Joseph Santley. With Ray Walker, Arline Judge, and Jimmy Fay. Unbilled.

Go into Your Dance (Warner Bros., 1935). Director: Archie L. Mayo. With Al Jolson, Ruby Keeler, and Glenda Farrell. As a thug.

Men of the Hour (Columbia, 1935). Director: Lambert Hillyer. With Richard Cromwell, Billie Seward, and Wallace Ford. As Joe.

After the Dance (Columbia, 1935). Director: Leo Bulgakov. With Nancy Carroll, George Murphy, and Thelma Todd. As Tom.

Don't Bet on Blondes (Warner Bros., 1935). Director: Robert Florey. With Warren William, Claire Dodd, and Guy Kibbee. As a gangster.

Little Big Shot (Warner Bros., 1935). Director: Michael Curtiz. With Sybil Jason, Glenda Farrell, and Robert Armstrong. As a henchman.

Dr. Socrates (Warner Bros., 1935). Director: William Dieterle. With Paul Muni, Ann Dvorak, and Barton MacLane. As Lefty.

Three Kids and a Queen (Universal, 1935). Director: Edward Ludwig. With May Robson, Henry Armetta, and Herman Bing. As a gangster.

Don't Gamble with Love (Columbia, 1936). Director: Dudley Murphy. With Ann Sothern, Bruce Cabot, and Irving Pichel. As a gambler.

Love on a Bet (RKO, 1936). Director: Leigh Jason. With Gene Raymond, Wendy Barrie, and Helen Broderick. Unbilled.

Road Gang (Warner Bros., 1936). Director: Louis King. With Donald Woods, Kay Linaker, and Carlyle Moore Jr. As Pete.

Robin Hood of El Dorado (M-G-M, 1936). Director: William A. Wellman. With Warner Baxter, Ann Loring, and Bruce Cabot. As Manuel.

Desire (Paramount, 1936). Director: Frank Borzage. With Marlene Dietrich, Gary Cooper, and John Halliday. Unbilled.

The Blackmailer (Columbia, 1936). Director: Gordon Wiles. With William Gargan, Florence Rice, and H. B. Warner. As Pinky.

Counterfeit (Columbia, 1936). Director: Erle C. Kenton. With Chester Morris, Margot Grahame, and Lloyd Nolan. As Dint Coleman.

Trapped by Television (Columbia, 1936). Director: Del Lord. With Mary Astor, Lyle Talbot, and Nat Pendleton. As Griffin.

The Final Hour (Columbia, 1936). Director: D. Ross Lederman. With Ralph Bellamy, Marguerite Churchill, and John Gallaudet. As Mike Magellon.

The Cowboy Star (Columbia, 1936). Director: David Selman. With Charles Starrett, Iris Meredith, and Si Jenks. As Johnny Simpson.

Night Waitress (RKO, 1936). Director: Lew Landers. With Margot Grahame, Gordon Jones, and Vinton Haworth. As Dom.

Racketeers in Exile (Columbia, 1937). Director: Erle C. Kenton. With George Bancroft, Evelyn Venable, and Wynne Gibson. As Blackie White.

Criminals of the Air (Columbia, 1937). Directors: C. C. Coleman Jr. and Folmer Blangsted. With Rosalind Keith, Charles Quigley, and Rita Hayworth. As Blast Reardon.

I Promise to Pay (Columbia, 1937). Director: D. Ross Lederman. With Chester Morris, Leo Carrillo, and Helen Mack. As Martin.

Motor Madness (Columbia, 1937). Director: D. Ross Lederman. With Rosalind Keith, Allen Brook, and Richard Terry. As Slater.

What Price Vengeance (Central Films/Columbia, 1937). Director: Del Lord. With Lyle Talbot, Wendy Barrie, and Eddie Acuff. As Peter Brower.

It Can't Last Forever (Columbia, 1937). Director: Hamilton MacFadden. With Ralph Bellamy, Betty Furness, and Robert Armstrong. Unbilled.

A Dangerous Adventure (Columbia, 1937). Director: D. Ross Lederman. With Don Terry, Rosalind Keith, and Nana Bryant. As Calkins.

San Quentin (Warner Bros., 1937). Director: Lloyd Bacon. With Pat O'Brien, Humphrey Bogart, and Ann Sheridan. As Venetti.

Counsel for Crime (Columbia, 1937). Director: John Brahm. With Otto Kruger, Douglass Montgomery, and Jacqueline Wells. As Edwin Mitchell.

Charlie Chan on Broadway (20th Century-Fox, 1937). Director: Eugene Forde. With Warner Oland, Keye Luke, and Joan Marsh. As Thomas Mitchell.

Life Begins with Love (Columbia, 1937). Director: Raymond B. McCarey. With Jean Peters, Douglass Montgomery, and Edith Fellowes. Unbilled.

Murder in Greenwich Village (Columbia, 1937). Director: Albert S. Rogell. With Richard Arlen, Fay Wray, and Raymond Walburn. As Rudy Morgan.

The Shadow (Columbia, 1937). Director: C. C. Coleman Jr. With Rita Hayworth, Charles Quigley, and Arthur Loft. As Kid Crow.

Penitentiary (Columbia, 1938). Director: John Brahm. With Walter Connolly, John Howard, and Jean Parker. As Jack Hawkins.

Squadron of Honor (Columbia, 1938). Director: C. C. Coleman Jr. With Don Terry, Mary Russell, and Thurston Hall. As Lawlor.

Who Killed Gail Preston? (Columbia, 1938). Director: Leon Barsha. With Don Terry, Rita Hayworth, and Robert Paige. As Frank Daniels.

Convicted (Central Films/Columbia, 1938). Director: Leon Barsha. With Charles Quigley, Rita Hayworth, and George McKay. As Milton Militis.

I Am the Law (Columbia, 1938). Director: Alexander Hall. With Edward G. Robinson, Barbara O'Neil, and John Beal. As Eddie Girard.

Adventure in Sahara (Columbia, 1938). Director: D. Ross Lederman. With Paul Kelly, C. Henry Gordon, and Lorna Gray. As Poule.

There's That Woman Again (Columbia, 1938). Director: Alexander Hall. With Melvyn Douglas, Virginia Bruce, and Margaret Lindsay. As Mr. Stevens.

The Spider's Web (Columbia, 1938). Directors: Ray Taylor and James W. Horne. With Warren Hull, Iris Meredith, and Richard Fiske. As Steve. A fifteen-chapter serial.

The Lone Wolf Spy Hunt (Columbia, 1939). Director: Peter Godfrey. With Warren William, Ida Lupino, and Rita Hayworth. As leader of the heavies.

While New York Sleeps (20th Century-Fox, 1939). Director: H. Bruce Humberstone. With Michael Whalen, Jean Rogers, and Chick Chandler. As Happy Nelson.

Homicide Bureau (Columbia, 1939). Director: C. C. Coleman Jr. With Bruce Cabot, Rita Hayworth, and Richard Fiske. As Chuck Brown.

Charlie Chan in Honolulu (20th Century-Fox, 1939). Director: H. Bruce Humberstone. With Sidney Toler, Phyllis Brook, and Sen Yung. As Johnny McCoy.

Romance of the Redwoods (Columbia, 1939). Director: Charles Vidor. With Charles Bickford, Jean Parker, and Alan Bridge. As Joe.

Sergeant Madden (M-G-M, 1939). Director: Josef von Sternberg.

With Wallace Beery, Tom Brown, and Alan Curtis. As "Piggy" Ceders.

Code of the Streets (Universal, 1939). Director: Harold Young. With Harry Carey, Frankie Thomas, and James McCallion. As Halstead.

Blind Alley (Columbia, 1939). Director: Charles Vidor. With Chester Morris, Ralph Bellamy, and Ann Dvorak. As Buck.

Ex-Champ (Universal, 1939). Director: Philip Rosen. With Victor McLaglen, Tom Brown, and Nan Grey. As Bill Crosley.

S.O.S.—Tidal Wave (Republic, 1939). Director: John H. Auer. With Ralph Byrd, George Barbier, and Kay Sutton. As Melvin Sutter.

Dust Be My Destiny (Warner Bros., 1939). Director: Lewis Seiler. With John Garfield, Priscilla Lane, and Alan Hale. As Venetti.

The Housekeeper's Daughter (Hal Roach/United Artists, 1939). Director: Hal Roach. With Joan Bennett, Adolphe Menjou, and John Hubbard. As Floyd.

Beware, Spooks! (Columbia, 1939). Director: Edward Sedgwick. With Joe E. Brown, Mary Carlisle, and Clarence Kolb. As Slick Eastman.

Invisible Stripes (Warner Bros., 1939). Director: Lloyd Bacon. With George Raft, Jane Bryan, and William Holden. As Lefty.

Johnny Apollo (20th Century-Fox, 1940). Director: Henry Hathaway. With Tyrone Power, Dorothy Lamour, and Edward Arnold. As Bates.

Love, Honor and Oh-Baby! (Universal, 1940). Director: Charles Lamont. With Wallace Ford, Mona Barrie, and Donald Woods. As Tony.

The Golden Fleecing (M-G-M, 1940). Director: Leslie Fenton. With Lew Ayres, Rita Johnson, and Lloyd Nolan. As "Happy" Dugan.

The Great Profile (20th Century-Fox, 1940). Director: Walter Lang. With John Barrymore, Mary Beth Hughes, and Gregory Ratoff. As Tony.

The Man Who Talked Too Much (Warner Bros., 1940). Director: Vincent Sherman. With George Brent, Virginia Bruce, and Brenda Marshall. As Lefty Kyler.

Brigham Young—Frontiersman (20th Century-Fox, 1940). Director: Henry Hathaway. With Tyrone Power, Linda Darnell, and Dean Jagger. As prosecutor.

Charlie Chan at the Wax Museum (20th Century-Fox, 1940). Director: Lynn Shores. With Sidney Toler, Sen Yung, and C. Henry Gordon. As Steve McBirney.

Tall, Dark and Handsome (20th Century-Fox, 1941). Director: H. Bruce Humberstone. With Cesar Romero, Virginia Gilmore, and Milton Berle. As Louie.

The Monster and the Girl (Paramount, 1941). Director: Stuart Heisler. With Ellen Drew, Rod Cameron, and Paul Lukas. As Sleeper.

A Dangerous Game (Universal, 1941). Director: John Rawlins. With Richard Arlen, Andy Devine, and Jeanne Kelly. As Joe.

Man Who Lost Himself (Universal, 1941). Director: Edward Ludwig. With Brian Aherne, Kay Francis, and Henry Stephenson. As Voles's man.

Blossoms in the Dust (M-G-M, 1941). Director: Mervyn LeRoy. With Greer Garson, Walter Pidgeon, and Feliz Bressart. As La Verne.

The Shepherd of the Hills (Paramount, 1941). Director: Henry Hathaway. With John Wayne, Betty Field, and Harry Carey. As Pete.

Lady Scarface (RKO, 1941). Director: Frank Woodruff. With Dennis O'Keefe, Judith Anderson, and Frances Neal. As Lefty Landers.

Hold That Ghost (Universal, 1941). Director: Arthur Lubin. With Bud Abbott, Lou Costello, and Richard Carlson. As Charlie Smith.

Sundown (Walter Wanger/United Artists, 1941). Director: Henry Hathaway. With Gene Tierney, Bruce Cabot, and George Sanders. As Hammond.

Public Enemies (Republic, 1942). Director: Albert S. Rogell. With Phillip Terry, Wendy Barrie, and Edgar Kennedy. As Mike.

This Gun for Hire (Paramount, 1942). Director: Frank Tuttle. With Veronica Lake, Robert Preston, and Laird Cregar. As Tommy.

Yokel Boy (Republic, 1942). Director: Joseph Santley. With Albert Dekker, Joan Davis, and Eddie Foy Jr. As Trigger.

Call of the Canyon (Republic, 1942). Director: Joseph Santley. With Gene Autry, Smiley Burnette, and the Sons of the Pioneers. As Horace Dunston.

Nazi Agent (M-G-M, 1942). Director: Jules Dassin. With Conrad Veidt, Ann Ayars, and Frank Reicher. As Joe Aiello.

Eyes of the Underworld (Universal, 1942). Director: Roy William Neill. With Richard Dix, Lon Chaney, and Wendy Barry. As Finch.

'Neath Brooklyn Bridge (Monogram, 1942). Director: Wallace Ford. With Leo Gorcey, Bobby Jordan, and Huntz Hall. As McGaffey.

The Ox-Bow Incident (20th Century-Fox, 1943). Director: William A. Wellman. With Henry Fonda, Dana Andrews, and Mary Beth Hughes. As Farnley.

Calaboose (Hal Roach/United Artists, 1943). Director: Glenn Tryon. With Jimmy Rogers, Noah Beery Jr., and Mary Brian. As Sluggsy Baker.

Submarine Alert (Pine-Thomas/Paramount, 1943). Director: Frank McDonald. With Richard Arlen, Wendy Barrie, and Nils Asther. As Vincent Belga.

Hit the Ice (Universal, 1943). Director: Charles Lamont. With Bud Abbott, Lou Costello, and Ginny Simms. As Phil.

Tampico (20th Century-Fox, 1944). Director: Lothar Mendes. With Edward G. Robinson, Lynn Bari, and Victor McLaglen. As Valdez.

Rainbow Island (Paramount, 1944). Director: Ralph Murphy. With Dorothy Lamour, Eddie Bracken, and Gil Lamb. As Alcoa.

The Princess and the Pirate (Samuel Goldwyn/United Artists, 1945). Director: David Butler. With Bob Hope, Virginia Mayo, and Walter Brennan. As Pedro.

Dillinger (King Brothers/Monogram, 1945). Director: Max Nosseck. With Edmund Lowe, Anne Jeffreys, and Laurence Tierney. As Doc.

Flame of the Barbary Coast (Republic, 1945). Director: Joseph Kane. With John Wayne, Ann Dvorak, and Joseph Schildkraut. As Disko.

Don't Fence Me In (Republic, 1945). Director: John English. With Roy Rogers, George "Gabby" Hayes, and Dale Evans. As Cliff Anson.

Club Havana (PRC, 1946). Director: Edgar G. Ulmer. With Tom Neal, Margaret Lindsay, and Don Douglas. As Joe Reed.

Life with Blondie (Columbia, 1946). Director: Abby Berlin. With Penny Singleton, Athur Lake, and Marjorie Kent. As Pete.

Blonde Alibi (Universal, 1946). Director: Will Jason. With Martha O'Driscoll, Tom Neal, and Donald MacBride. As Joe Di Lima.

The Virginian (Paramount, 1946). Director: Stuart Gilmore. With Joel McCrea, Brian Donlevy, and Sonny Tufts. As Pete.

Cloak and Dagger (Warner Bros., 1946). Director: Fritz Lang. With Gary Cooper, Lilli Palmer, and Robert Alda. As Luigi.

Unconquered (Paramount, 1947). Director: Cecil B. DeMille. With Gary Cooper, Paulette Goddard, and Howard Da Silva. As Sloto, the medicine man.

Yankee Fakir (Republic, 1947). Director: W. Lee Wilder. With Douglas Fowley, Joan Woodbury, and Clem Bevans. As Duke.

Captain from Castille (20th Century-Fox, 1947). Director: Henry King. With Tyrone Power, Jean Peters, and Cesar Romero. As Corio.

Joe Palooka in the Knockout (Monogram, 1947). Director: Reginald Le Borg. With Joe Kirkwood, Leon Errol, and Morris Carnovsky. Unbilled.

I Walk Alone (Paramount, 1948). Director: Byron Haskin. With Burt Lancaster, Lizabeth Scott, and Kirk Douglas. As Nick Palesto.

Key Largo (Warner Bros., 1948). Director: John Huston. With Humphrey Bogart, Edward G. Robinson, and Lauren Bacall. As Ziggy.

Out of the Storm (Republic, 1948). Director: R. G. Springsteen. With James Lydon, Lois Collier, and Richard Travis. As Red Stubbins.

Jigsaw (Danziger/United Artists, 1949). Director: Fletcher Markle. With Franchot Tone, Jean Wallace, and Myron McCormick. As Angelo Agostini.

Calamity Jane and Sam Bass (Universal-International, 1949). Director: George Sherman. With Yvonne DeCarlo, Howard Duff, and Dorothy Hart. As Dean.

Tough Assignment (Lippert, 1949). Director: William Beaudine. With Don Barry, Marjorie Steele, and Steve Brodie. As Vince.

Black Hand (M-G-M, 1950). Director: Richard Thorpe. With Gene Kelly, J. Carroll Naish, and Teresa Celli. As Cesar Xavier Serpi.

The Asphalt Jungle (M-G-M, 1950). Director: John Huston. With Sterling Hayden, Louis Calhern, and Jean Hagen. As Cobby.

Abbott and Costello in the Foreign Legion (Universal-International, 1950). Director: Charles Lamont. With Bud Abbott, Lou Costello, and Patricia Medina. As Frankie.

The Desert Hawk (Universal-International, 1950). Director: Frederick de Cordova. With Yvonne DeCarlo, Richard Greene, and Jackie Gleason. As Samad.

Hurricane Island (Columbia, 1951). Director: Lew Landers. With Jon Hall, Marie Windsor, and Romo Vincent. As Angus Macready.

My Favorite Spy (Paramount, 1951). Director: Norman Z. McLeod. With Bob Hope, Hedy Lamarr, and Francis L. Sullivan. As Ben Ali.

Vacanze col Gangster (Holidays with a Gangster) (Mambretti/Lux, 1951). Director: Dino Risi. With Lamberto Maggiorani, Guido Pala, and Massimo Girotti.

Tormento del Passato (Torment of the Past) (EDIC, 1952). Director: Mario Bonnard. With Carla de Poggio, Helene Remy, and Carlo Romano.

Noi Peccatori (We Sinners) (Titanus, 1952). Director: Guido Brignone. With Carla de Poggio, Frank Latimore, and Gabrielle Fezetti. Released in the United States in 1960 by William Mishkin as *The Naked and the Wicked*.

I Tre Corsari (The Three Pirates) (Ponti-De Laurentiis, 1952). Director: Mario Soldati. With Ettore Manni, Barbara Florian, and Mai Britt.

Iolanda, la Figlia del Corsaro Nero (Iolanda, Daughter of the Black Pirate) (Ponti-De Laurentiis, 1952). Director: Mario Soldati. With Barbara Florian, Umberto Spadaro, and Cesare Danova. As Morgan the pirate.

La Tratta Della Bianche (Ponti-De Laurentiis-Excelsa-Minerva/IFE, 1953). Director: Luigi Comencini. With Vittorio Gassman, Eleanora Rossi-Drago, and Silvana Pampanini. As Marquedi. Released in the United States in 1954 as *Girls Marked Danger*.

Helen of Troy (Warner Bros., 1955). Director: Robert Wise. With Rossana Podesta, Jacques Sernas, and Sir Cedric Hardwicke. As Diomedes.

Kill Her Gently (Fortress/Columbia, 1958). Director: Charles Saunders. With George Mikell, Griffith Jones, and John Grayford. As William Connors.

Johnny Cool (Chrislaw/United Artists, 1963). Dirctor: William Asher. With Henry Silva, Elizabeth Montgomery, and Richard Anderson. As Johnny Colini.

Nightmare in the Sun (Afilmco/Zociac Films, 1964). Director: Marc Lawrence. With Ursula Andress, John Derek, and Aldo Ray.

Johnny Tiger (Nova-Hugh/Universal, 1966). Director: Paul Wendkos. With Robert Taylor, Geraldine Brooks, and Chad Everett. As William Billie.

Due Mafiosi Contro Al Capone (Fida-Atlantida, 1966). Director: Georgio Simonelli. With Franco Franchi, Ciccio Ingrassia, and Jose Calvo.

Du Mou Dans la Gachette (Rivers, 1967). Director: Louis Grospierre. With Bertrand Blier, Jean Lefebvre, and Francis Blanche.

Savage Pampas (Samuel Bronston-Dasa Films-Jamie Prades/ Comet, 1967). Director: Hugo Fregonese. With Robert Taylor, Ron Randell, and Ty Hardin. As Sergeant Barril.

Custer of the West (Security Pictures/Cinerama, 1968). Director: Robert Siodmak. With Robert Shaw, Mary Ure, and Jeffrey Hunter. As the gold miner.

Krakatoa, East of Java (Security Pictures/Cinerama, 1969). Director: Bernard L. Kowalski. With Maximillian Schell, Diane Baker, and Brian Keith. As Jacobs.

The Five Man Army (Tiger/M-G-M, 1970). Director: Don Taylor. With Peter Graves, James Daly, and Bud Spencer. As carnival barker.

The Kremlin Letter (20th Century-Fox, 1970). Director: John Huston. With Bibi Anderson, Richard Boone, and Nigel Green. As a priest.

Diamonds Are Forever (Albert Broccoli-Harry Saltzman/United Artists, 1971). Director: Guy Hamilton. With Sean Connery, Jill St. John, and Charles Gray. As Gangster No. 1.

Frazier, The Sensuous Lion (Shuster-Sandler/LCS Distributing, 1973). Director: Pat Shields. With Michael Callan, Katherine Justice, and Victor Jory. As Chiarelli.

The Man with the Golden Gun (Albert Broccoli-Harry Saltzman/ United Artists, 1974). Director: Guy Hamilton. With Roger Moore, Christopher Lee, and Britt Ekland. As Rodney.

Marathon Man (Paramount, 1976). Director: John Schlesinger. With Dustin Hoffman, Laurence Olivier, and Roy Scheider. As Erhard.

A Piece of the Action (First Artists/Warner Bros., 1977). Director: Sidney Poitier. With Sidney Poitier, Bill Cosby, and James Earl Jones. As Louie.

Foul Play (Paramount, 1978). Director: Colin Higgins. With Goldie Hawn, Chevy Chase, and Burgess Meredith. As Stiltskin.

Goin' Coconuts (Osmond-Inter Planetary Pictures, 1978). Director: Howard Morris. With Donny Osmond, Marie Osmond, and Herbert Edelman. As Webster.

Dream No Evil (Boxoffice International, 1978). Director: John Hayes. With Edmond O'Brien, Brooke Mills, and Michael Pataki. As undertaker.

Hot Stuff (Rastar-Mort Engleberg/Columbia, 1979). Director: Dom DeLuise. With Dom DeLuise, Jerry Reed, and Suzanne Pleshette. As Carmine.

Cataclysm (First International Pictures/Vista International, 1979). Director: John Carr. With John Phillip Law, Cameron Mitchell, and Charles Moll. As Weiss/Dieter. Released in 1985 as *Night Train to Terror*.

Super Fuzz (Transcinema-TV Inc/Avco Embassy, 1981). Director: Sergio Corbucci. With Terence Hill, Ernest Borgnine, and Joanne Dru. As Tropedo.

Daddy's Deadly Darling (D&R-Safia/Aquarius Releasing, 1984). Director: Marc Lawrence. With Toni Lawrence, Jesse Vint, and Walter Barnes. As Zambrini. Also known as *The Pigs* and *Daddy's Girl*.

The Big Easy (Kings Road Entertainment/Columbia, 1986). Director: Jim McBride. With Dennis Quaid, Ellen Barkin, and Ned Beatty. As Vinnie DiMoti.

Newsies (Walt Disney, 1992). Director: Kenny Ortega. With Christian Bale, Bill Pullman, and Ann-Margret. As Kloppman.

Ruby (Propaganda Films/Polygram, 1992). Director: John Mackenzie. With Danny Aiello, Sherilyn Fenn, and Tobin Bell. As Santos Alicante.

Life with Mikey (Touchstone/Buena Vista, 1993). Director: James Lapine. With Michael J. Fox, Christina Vidal, and Nathan Lane. Coproducer.

Four Rooms (A Band Apart/Miramax, 1995). Directors: Allison Anders, Alexandre Rockwell, Robert Rodrigues, and Quentin

Tarantino. With Tim Roth, Antonio Banderas, and Jennifer Beals. As Sam the bellhop.

From Dusk to Dawn (A Band Apart-Los Halligans/Dimension Pictures, 1996). Director: Robert Rodriguez. With George Clooney, Quentin Tarantino, and Harvey Keitel. As Old-timer.

Doris Nolan

The Man I Marry (Universal, 1936). Director: Ralph Murphy. With Michael Whalen, Charles "Chic" Sale, and Nigel Bruce. As Rena Allen.

Top of the Town (Universal, 1937). Director: Ralph Murphy. With George Murphy, Ella Logan, and Hugh Herbert. As Diana Borden.

As Good As Married (Universal, 1937). Director: Edward Buzzell. With John Boles, Walter Pidgeon, and Alan Mowbray. As Sylvia Parker.

Holiday (Columbia, 1938). Director: George Cukor. With Katharine Hepburn, Cary Grant, and Lew Ayres. As Julie Seton.

One Hour to Live (Universal, 1939). Director: Harold Schuster. With Charles Bickford, John Litel, and Samuel S. Hinds. As Muriel Vance.

Irene (RKO, 1940). Director: Herbert Wilcox. With Anna Neagle, Ray Milland, and Roland Young. As Lillian.

Moon over Burma (Paramount, 1940). Director: Louis King. With Dorothy Lamour, Robert Preston, and Preston Foster. As Cynthia Harmon.

Follies Girl (William Rowland/PRC, 1943). Director: William Rowland. With Wendy Barrie, Gordon Oliver, and Anne Barrett. As Francine La Rue.

The Servant (Springbok-Elstree/Warner Bros., 1963). Director: Joseph Losey. With Dirk Bogarde, Sarah Miles, and Wendy Craig. As older lesbian in restaurant.

Juggernaut (Richard de Koker/United Artists, 1974). Director: Richard Lester. With Richard Harris, Omar Sharif, and David Hemmings. As Mrs. Corrigan.

The Romantic Englishwoman (Dial Meric-Matalon/New World, 1975). Director: Joseph Losey. With Glenda Jackson, Michael Caine, and Helmut Berger. As Thomas's older woman friend.

INDEX

ABOUT THE AUTHOR

Anthony Slide is no stranger to interviews and oral histories. Since 1971, when he first came to the United States from his native England as a Louis B. Mayer Research Associate with the American Film Institute, he has conducted literally hundreds of interviews, now on deposit with the Academy of Motion Picture Arts and Sciences, the University of Southern California, and elsewhere. His 1996 book of interviews with director Andre de Toth, *De Toth on De Toth* (published by Faber and Faber), was among Amazon.com's top ten film books of the year.

The former resident film historian of the Academy of Motion Pictures Arts and Sciences, Anthony Slide is the author or editor of more than sixty books on the history of popular entertainment including *The Films of D. W. Griffith, The Encyclopedia of Vaudeville, The Silent Feminists: America's First Women Directors,* and *The New Historical Dictionary of the American Film Industry.* He is also editor of the Scarecrow Press "Filmmakers" series, and for the past ten years he has written a monthly book review column in *Classic Images.*

In 1990, in recognition of his work on the history of popular entertainment, Anthony Slide was awarded a honorary doctorate of letters by Bowling Green University. At that time, he was hailed by Lillian Gish as "our pre-eminent historian of the silent film."